# Your Words Have Power

*Also by R. T. Kendall*

The Anointing
The Christian and the Pharisee (with David Rosen)
The Gift of Giving
Great Christian Prayers
(compiled and edited by Louise Kendall)
In Pursuit of His Glory
Out of the Comfort Zone
Pure Joy
Tales of Total Forgiveness (with Julia Fisher)
Thanking God
The Sensitivity of the Spirit
The Thorn in the Flesh
Total Forgiveness
Worshipping God

# Your Words Have Power

## Controlling the Tongue

### R. T. Kendall

HODDER &
STOUGHTON

Copyright © 2006 by R. T. Kendall

First published in Great Britain in 2006

Reprinted 2007

The right of R. T. Kendall to be identified as the Author of the
Work has been asserted by him in accordance with the Copyright,
Designs and Patents Act 1988.

British Library Cataloguing in Publication Data
A record for this book is available from the British Library

ISBN 978 0340 910177

Typeset in Bembo by Avon DataSet Ltd,
Bidford on Avon, Warwickshire

Printed in the UK by CPI Bookmarque, Croydon, CR0 4TD

The paper and board used in this paperback are natural recyclable
products made from wood grown in sustainable forests.
The manufacturing processes conform to the environmental
regulations of the country of origin.

Hodder & Stoughton
A Division of Hodder Headline Ltd
338 Euston Road
London NW1 3BH
www.hodderchristianbooks.com

*To Kieran and Beryl Grogan*

# Contents

| | | |
|---|---|---|
| Preface | | ix |
| Foreword by Lyndon Bowring | | xi |
| Introduction | | 1 |
| | | |
| | Part One: Failure in Tongue Control | 9 |
| 1 | Pointing the Finger | 11 |
| 2 | Self-pity | 17 |
| 3 | Manipulating Providence | 25 |
| 4 | Trying to Prove Ourselves | 31 |
| 5 | Speaking out of Fear | 37 |
| 6 | Losing your Temper | 41 |
| 7 | Lust | 45 |
| | | |
| | Part Two: Success in Controlling the Tongue | 53 |
| 8 | Climbing Down | 59 |
| 9 | In the Presence of an Enemy | 73 |
| 10 | Dignifying the Trial | 85 |

11  Total Forgiveness                                           99

    Part Three: The Trouble with the Tongue          107
12  The Tongue on the Way to Church                    111
13  Asking for Trouble                                        117
14  The Proof of Self-control                               123
15  The Dangerous Potential of the Tongue            129
16  The Fire of Hell                                            137
17  Poison                                                         147

    Part Four: Motivation to Change                      157
18  Scandalous Worship                                       159
19  Meeting Another's N-E-E-D                            167
20  The Positive Power of the Tongue                   181
21  Laughing at Ourselves – When we Fear           193
    we've Blown it

    Conclusion                                                   207

# Preface

There is a rather funny (if a little complicated) story that lies behind the making and the title of this book. When I was asked to list all my books at the end of *In Pursuit of His Glory* (Hodder & Stoughton, 2002), the account of my twenty-five years at Westminster Chapel, I put my chosen title, *Controlling the Tongue*, for the second volume on the book of James, which at the time was not yet published. But when it emerged from the press I noticed the British publisher (Paternoster) called it *The Way of Wisdom*.

I gave it no more thought until my American publisher asked me to do my book *Controlling the Tongue* – which they picked out from the list in *In Pursuit of His Glory*. I pointed out that this book was an exposition of James 3–5 and was possibly not what they were wanting. So they asked, 'Would you then do a book on "Controlling the Tongue"?' I agreed to this and it will be published in the United States under that title.

But when I submitted this same book to Hodder & Stoughton, they did not like the title *Controlling the Tongue*. It therefore seems that British publishers really don't like this title! Although this book will be called *Controlling the Tongue* in America, it comes to you in Britain as *Your Words Have Power*. It is one of those interesting differences between Brits and Americans! The point is, were it not for this strange scenario, the present book would not have been printed at all!

I thank David Moloney of Hodder & Stoughton for his wise counsel and for publishing this book. I also thank Cecilia Moore for the hard work she and the copy editor have done to fine-tune what I have written.

I am grateful to my very close friend Lyndon Bowring for writing the Foreword. If you were to delete Lyndon's influence on my life during the last twenty years, it would leave a gap so big that I would be unrecognisable today. Thank you, Lyndon, for your trust and friendship.

This book is dedicated to Kieran and Beryl Grogan. Kieran was our worship leader in my final years at Westminster Chapel, and Beryl was my secretary. These two have remained close friends and a book dedicated to them is long overdue.

Most of all, I thank my wife Louise, my best friend and wisest critic, for her role in the making of this book. May God bless you as you read it.

R. T. Kendall
April 2006
Key Largo, Florida
www.rtkendallministries.com

# Foreword

I have known R.T. for over twenty years. He is an exceedingly close and treasured friend and my understanding
of Scripture, and God's purposes for my own life, has
been immeasurably enriched by my close friendship with
him.

One of the many things I admire about R.T. is that he is
not ashamed to expose his greatest failures and weaknesses,
to search for ways to overcome them and then seek to work
it out daily in his own experience. He is a man who not
only loves the truth but longs with all his heart to 'walk the
talk' and then preach it!

This book is vintage R.T. 'warts 'n all'. His sound biblical
and practical remedies for the problems of the tongue are
fantastic. For someone whose words in preaching and
writing are his life's calling it may surprise you to discover
how much R.T., like the rest of us, has also always struggled
with the misuse of the tongue. I couldn't put the manuscript

down and as I read, became aware afresh of a growing hunger and thirst for righteousness and holiness in my own heart and ever-increasing desire for purity in my thoughts and speech.

It seems an age since I have 'heard' preaching like this and so I wholeheartedly commend this book to you. By taking its principles to heart and calling on God's highest willingness to help us, each one of us can resolve to control our tongue and increasingly speak words that are edifying to others and glorifying to God.

I cannot thank God enough for what you are about to read. Prepare to be challenged, informed, convicted, enlightened and shown the way of the Spirit – the pathway of love and self-control.

Lyndon Bowring
2006

# 1

# Introduction

The wisdom that comes from heaven is first of all pure; then peace-loving, considerate, submissive, full of mercy and good fruit, impartial and sincere.

*Js 3:17*

I don't write on this subject because I'm an expert on it – or because I have mastered control of my own tongue. That would be like writing the book 'Humility and How I Attained it'!

Quite the contrary. I write this because I have made nearly *every mistake imaginable* in this area. I have been in the ministry for over fifty years. I am now seventy. When you reach my age you take life, health and death more seriously than in earlier years. I know one thing for sure: I want to make every remaining moment count, especially knowing that 'we must all appear before the judgment seat of Christ, that each one may receive what is due to him

for the things done while in the body, whether good or bad'
(2 Cor. 5:10). At that time God will 'bring to light what is
hidden in darkness and will expose the motives of men's
hearts. At that time each will receive his praise from God'
(1 Cor. 4:5).

So as you get older you think more and more about the
remaining years and how it will be at the Final Judgement.

Could I give you what is perhaps my most 'unfavourite'
verse in the Bible? It is Matthew 12:36 – the words of Jesus,
'I tell you that men will have to give account on the day of
judgment for every careless word they have spoken.'

A careless word. 'Idle word' (KJV). 'Useless word' (TEV).
'Thoughtless word' (NEB). Oh dear. I am in serious trouble.
This does not make me look forward to the Day of
Judgement.

I cannot think of anything scarier than having every
careless word, idle word, useless word or thoughtless word
thrown up at me on that Day. Imagine this: you are standing before the Lord with him looking on, but also everybody else (this is also why it hurts so much). I don't know
how it will happen – whether God gives earphones to
everybody to eavesdrop our conversations – in secret and in
public. I only know this is a word that I take seriously, and
so should you. Were we to believe it literally, I can assure
you that it would go a long way in helping us to control
our tongues!

Consider the wisdom of these words: 'Do not revile the
king even in your thoughts, or curse the rich in your
bedroom, because a bird of the air may carry your words,
and a bird on the wing may report what you say' (Eccles.
10:20). As I hope there will be no wasted words in this
book, so too do I hope that in my life – in public and in

private, in the pulpit or with friends, with family or with strangers – I may make very few unguarded comments that I will have to listen to one day before all people.

## Definitions

Before we proceed further we must define some terms, even if we think we already know what they mean. Controlling the tongue is self-restraint with words, having *the wisdom to know what to say* – and saying it, but equally knowing when *not* to speak – and saying nothing. Wisdom, or the lack of it, is what lies behind our conversations. This is why James 3:17, bringing to a conclusion his well-known discourse on the tongue, says:

> The *wisdom* that comes from heaven is first of all pure, then peace-loving, considerate, submissive, full of mercy and good fruit, impartial and sincere.

Wisdom may be defined in two ways: both generally and particularly. The general definition embraces several words: intelligence, insight, discernment, unusual knowledge and ability – all of which are derived from the *fear of the Lord*. The first step toward finding true wisdom therefore is to fear the Lord: 'the fear of the Lord is the beginning of wisdom' (Prov. 9:10). Wisdom is sometimes used inter-changeably with understanding. 'Wisdom is supreme; therefore get wisdom. Though it cost all you have [whatever else you get], get understanding' (Prov. 4:7). The word *understanding* in Hebraic thinking meant insight as a gift of God. Not what one is born with or possesses naturally but what the Lord bestows.

Like it or not, the only way to get true wisdom is to fear the Lord. A person may be born with a great intellect and not have wisdom. One may have great education and learning but not have wisdom. 'Clever but not wise' is a phrase that may describe many a person with a high profile in politics, education, government, business, finance and also the ministry. The first step towards wisdom, therefore, is putting your relationship with God right, respecting him and his word, and making his honour your priority.

This is very important. If you and I are to enjoy tongue control, we cannot bypass the most crucial and foundational principle of all: the fear of the Lord. Let no reader of this book delude himself or herself with the thought that you can pick up some 'tips' on how to control the tongue by reading this book and at the same time ignore the fear of the Lord. This is not a secular book, it is not a 'how to' book for people who are not interested in God or his word. With deepest respect, you are a fool if you fancy learning how to control the tongue when there is not an underlying fear of God in your very being.

We never outgrow the fear of the Lord in the Christian life. It was the fear of the Lord that brought about our conversion in the first place. As the second line of the famous hymn 'Amazing Grace' put it,

> 'Twas grace that taught my heart to fear, and grace my fears relieved;
> How precious did that grace appear the hour I first believed!
>
> *John Newton (1725–1807)*

We must never think, for example, that we can outgrow

4

asking God for mercy. We were initially converted by saying, 'God, have mercy on me, a sinner' – or the equivalent words (Luke 18:13). Yet the most mature Christian still comes daily to the throne of Grace to receive 'mercy' (Heb. 4:16). So too with the fear of God: we must never, never, never think we should outgrow the deepest respect and sense of awe toward God Almighty.

There is, however, a difference between the fear of God and the spirit of fear. God has not given us a spirit of fear, or timidity or anxiety (2 Tim. 1:7). A spirit of fear leads to the opposite of tongue control. As a matter of fact, a spirit of fear produces what James calls *false wisdom* – that which is 'earthly, unspiritual, of the devil' (Js 3:15). A spirit of fear always leads to evil (Ps. 37:8).

A spirit of fear is overcome by a true fear of God – a care to please him in all our ways. This care to please him is what leads to wisdom. You will not even come close to controlling the tongue if you dismiss these lines. Only the fear of the Lord leads to true wisdom. Wisdom therefore is the key to self-control. The fruit of the Spirit is self-control (Gal. 5:23). This then is what I mean by a general definition of wisdom.

A particular definition of wisdom is knowing what to do next and having the ability to carry it out. Particular wisdom therefore is knowing what is the next step forward. We should all pray for this kind of wisdom every day. So too with controlling the tongue, or self-restraint with words. Wisdom with the tongue is knowing what to say next – and saying it; and having the self-discipline *not to speak* when you have the presence of mind that keeping your mouth shut truly is the next step forward. Controlling the tongue is having the presence of mind what to say, what not to say; saying what is wise, not speaking at all when this is wise.

James puts our minds at ease when he says that if we are never at fault in what we say, we are *perfect* (Js 3:2). But none of us is perfect! As the New Living Translation put it, 'Those who control their tongues can also control themselves in every other way.' Tongue control is a noble goal; it leads to self-discipline in every area of our lives.

We will never be perfect in this life. This is because we always have our fallen nature with us. 'The heart is deceitful above all things and beyond cure. Who can understand it?' (Jer. 17:9). What we inherited from our first parents in the Garden of Eden we will have until we are glorified, when we are totally changed (1 Cor. 15:51). Until then we are conscious of indwelling sin, the propensity to impure thoughts, unguarded comments, imperfections that keep embarrassing us and weaknesses that reveal we have not been glorified yet. Until then we will err.

But that does not mean we do not try to be and do better! It is being a Christian that makes one want to get it right. This is one of the big differences between the Christian and the non-Christian. We have a motivation to be more like Jesus. We want to please God more and more. We want a greater testimony before others — saved and lost. Because we *can indeed improve*! I think of John Newton's words to his friend William Cowper, when they were discussing Paul's words, 'But by the grace of God I am what I am, and his grace to me was not without effect' (1 Cor. 15:10). Newton looked across the breakfast table at Cowper and said:

I'm not what I ought to be. I'm not what I want to be. I'm not what I hope to be. But thank God I'm not what I used to be.

The ultimate proof of words spoken in wisdom is Scripture itself. Our doctrine of the inspiration of the Bible comes into focus here. I believe in the infallibility of Holy Scripture, that it is totally inspired by the Holy Spirit – from Genesis to Revelation. This is because 'all Scripture is God-breathed and is useful for teaching, rebuking, correcting and training in righteousness, so that the man of God may be thoroughly equipped for every good work' (2 Tim. 3:16–17). The origin of Scripture is not in man, but 'men spoke from God as they were carried along by the Holy Spirit' (2 Pet. 1:21).

I write this book to encourage you. You will see you are not alone in losing control with the tongue. We all have this problem. I also write this book to challenge you. One of the greatest challenges we face is to master the tongue. I do believe this book can make a difference in your own life. That is the main purpose in writing it. I pray this book will change your life, that it will mark a turning point in your pilgrimage – that it will lead to your receiving a reward at the Judgement Seat of Christ. As we will see more clearly later, what Jesus said in Matthew 12:36 is not a reference to whether you are saved or lost but whether you receive a reward as a Christian on that Day.

I blush to think of the words I have uttered, the gossip I listened to and help spread, the things I have said in order to discredit my enemies, the language I have used when I lost my temper, not to mention what people remember – whether or not there may be some plausible explanation for my ill-chosen utterances. Once we've said it, whether in public, in private or in print — it is *done*. People don't forget.

> The moving finger writes and having writ, moves on;
> Not all your piety nor wit
> Shall lure it back to cancel half a line,
> Nor all your tears wash out a word of it.
>
> *Omar Khayyam (1048–1122)*

# Part One
# Failure in Tongue Control

> Now these things occurred as examples to keep us from
> setting our hearts on evil things as they did.
>
> *1 Cor. 10:6*

Another way of understanding controlling the tongue is by
seeing examples of what self-restraint with words most certainly is not. We will do this in the present chapter by
examining biblical examples – when people in the Old and
New Testaments failed to show wisdom and, in the following chapter, when they got it right.

The infallible word of God describes fallible men and
women between its covers. What Scripture says about them
we can believe, but what some of them *did* and *said* at times
was very often wrong. So even the best of God's servants
described in the Bible frequently turn out to be examples of

how *not* to be! Never forget that God records the bad that they did 'as examples to keep us from setting our hearts on evil things as they did' (1 Cor. 10:6). In other words, we don't need to repeat the same mistakes!

I have lived long enough to observe that every person I began to admire a little bit too much disappointed me sooner or later. We may wish that we lived in Bible times – and witnessed first hand some of the great people in biblical history – Abraham, Isaac, Jacob, David, Elijah, for example, and found out what they were really like; but you would have been shocked to see how human they were. They were not perfect. The imperfection was almost always traceable to the tongue.

What we say reveals the heart. 'Out of the overflow of the heart the mouth speaks' (Matt. 12:34). This is why Jesus said by our *words* we are either 'acquitted' or 'condemned' (Matt. 12:37) when the verdict is given as to our reward at the Judgement Seat of Christ. Our words, which reveal to what extent we truly sought after true wisdom, therefore indicate what was in the heart.

We now turn to some biblical examples. We will examine various categories of verbal sin and see people, some of them among God's best, who failed in the matter of controlling the tongue. What we now examine therefore are examples of *how not to be*. We will do this by observing typical sins we have all committed, at least to some degree; they reveal various weaknesses and typical failures in controlling the tongue. All these have their origin in our fallen nature.

# 1

# Pointing the Finger

You, therefore, have no excuse, you who pass judgment on someone else, for at whatever point you judge the other, you are condemning yourself, because you who pass judgment do the same things.

*Rom. 2:1*

The prophet Isaiah promised ancient Israel that the break-through they were hoping for – namely, that God would show up – would never come until certain conditions were met. These conditions included doing away with 'the yoke of oppression, with the pointing finger and malicious talk' (Isa. 58:9). When people are constantly blaming each other, no breakthrough is likely to come.

Blaming one another is a very natural practice. It is certainly not the working of the Holy Spirit. It springs from nature. It takes no education or training on 'how to learn to point the finger'. This practice comes straight out of the

Garden of Eden immediately after our first parents sinned. They started it and all of us have been doing it ever since.

1. *Adam, blaming God and his wife Eve immediately after his sin in the Garden of Eden.*

The first conversation God had with Adam after the Fall in the Garden of Eden finds Adam blaming not himself but his wife Eve for his partaking of the forbidden fruit. But if you look closely at these words you will see that Adam was actually pointing the finger at God himself. 'The woman *you* put here with me – she gave me some fruit from the tree, and I ate it' (Gen. 3:12). This was a dead giveaway that depravity had taken hold in Adam's heart. Corruption and vileness of the human heart has been with every man, every woman, every child – of all races, cultures and colours – ever since. Instinctively we do not see our own sin but that of others. We want to blame God, then others – but never ourselves if we can help it.

One of the irrefutable proofs that we are sinners is that we want to defend ourselves, shift the blame to someone else and avoid as long as possible the matter of admitting to our guilt. Essential to our natural depravity is self-righteousness. We were born with it. We did not need to attend Harvard or Oxford to learn how to be self-righteous. It is the most natural inclination in the world! It is intrinsic to our nature.

Adam revealed that sin had set in already when God came looking for him in the Garden of Eden, asking 'Where are you?' (Gen. 3:9). Adam did not want to face God and own his own guilt. Trying to shift the blame when it is our own fault is evidence of our sin of self-righteousness. Pointing the finger also shows we have lost control of the tongue.

We all have these evil thoughts. No matter how mature we become in the Christian faith evil thoughts will emerge in our hearts. Why? Because we are imperfect. I say it again, we will not be perfect until we are glorified and are changed to be like Jesus (1 John 3:3; Rom. 8:30). In the meantime vile thoughts enter our minds – we sometimes want to lash out at God or others, 'Why did you do this to me? Why did you let this happen?'

Controlling the tongue is having the wisdom not to say everything that enters our minds, including what we say to God. Yes, God knows we have these thoughts. He knows too when *we refuse to say* what enters our brains. He applauds us when we show wisdom.

You may say, 'But if you have the thought you might as well say it since God knows what you are thinking.' Wrong. Don't *say* it. Wisdom is self-control, not least when you talk to God. 'By your *words* [not what you may momentarily *think*] you will be condemned' (Matt. 12:37). It is what we *say* that gets us into trouble. Here is a prayer you and I cannot pray too often:

> May the words of my mouth and the meditation of my heart be pleasing in your sight, O Lord, my Rock and my Redeemer.
>
> Ps. 19:14

Or think about these words:

> Do not be quick with your mouth, do not be hasty in your heart to utter anything before God. God is in heaven and you are on earth, so let your words be few.'
>
> Eccles. 5:2

2. *Jacob, verbally abusing his own children.*

Jacob was the expert in pointing the finger. He loved to blame others, especially his sons. He did this with Simeon and Levi. Instead of giving them credit for wanting to preserve the honour of his daughter Dinah, he only thought of how he would appear to others:

> You have brought trouble on me by making me a stench to the Canaanites and Perizzites, the people living in this land.
>
> Gen. 34:30

Jacob even blamed his sons for the fact that the Prime Minister of Egypt demanded to see Benjamin. 'Why did you bring this trouble on me by telling him that you had another brother?' (Gen. 43:6).

Jacob is arguably the worst parent who ever lived. He showed favouritism by giving undue attention to Joseph and blamed the others sons for his own sense of guilt. He was the expert in making them feel guilty. It is like my friend who often says, 'My mother was a travel agent; she sends people on guilt trips.' Jacob did that all the time.

It is our *words* that make the difference. It is what our children *hear* that affects them. We may have thoughts – which may or may not be true, but when we utter them the damage is done.

In my book *In Pursuit of His Glory* (Charisma House), an account of my twenty-five years as Minister of Westminster Chapel, London, I close with a section, 'If I could turn the clock back' – and refer to how I would have put my family first, not my ministry, had I those years to live over again. But I could have added volumes to that. I feel I have made

14

almost every mistake that can be made when it comes to sending our children on guilt trips. I am too much like Jacob.

I don't want this book to send you on a guilt trip. We have all failed. These lines are from a mature minister of God who is trying to pass on a bit of wisdom to the next generation. Read on, I will deal with guilt over regrettable words too before the end of this book. But if there are those who read this who can put things right by ceasing to blame people – your children, your spouse, your friends, those around you – this book will be worth its weight in gold.

3. *Sarah, blaming Abraham for Hagar and Ishmael.*
'You are responsible for the wrong I am suffering' (Gen. 16:5). But it was Sarah's own suggestion that he sleep with Hagar, her maidservant, in order that Sarah could 'build a family through her' (Gen. 16:2). The result of this union was that Hagar gave birth to Ishmael. This caused immense problems in the household.

Once we realise we have made a wrong decision our self-righteous nature often lures us into thinking it was not our fault – but someone else's. So we blame others. We do this because we feel so guilty ourselves. Those who carry the greatest sense of guilt are brilliant in giving guilt trips. Or, to put it the other way around, those who give the greatest guilt trips usually have the deepest sense of guilt themselves. We foolishly think that pointing the finger is going to shift the blame and make us feel better.

Many marriages could be healed overnight if both the husband and the wife would *stop pointing the finger*. It is our words that make the other person feel bad. If we could stop keeping a record of wrongs in our marriage we would be miles ahead. Love 'keeps no record of wrongs' (1 Cor. 13:5). Why do we keep records? To prove that we paid, to prove we said this, promised that. But love will tear the records up – so they cannot be referred to again. But when we *keep* the record of the wrong it is because in that moment we have already decided to refer to it one day. 'I will remember that – I won't forget that,' the husband says to the wife. And he keeps his word. The marriage could be on the rocks.

Abraham and Sarah survived. But her pointing the finger put a severe strain on their marriage. It shows that the best of God's servants have marriage and family problems. But so many of them could be avoided if we stopped playing the blame game.

# 2

# Self-pity

Everything is against me!

*Gen. 42:36*

Self-pity is feeling sorry for yourself. You feel that you are
the object of unfair treatment, that you have had to carry a
load that few, if any, understand or appreciate. You perhaps
feel you were unlucky with having the parents you had, the
environment you grew up in, the education you received.
You may have been abused by an authority figure, lied
about, rejected and discriminated against. Whenever you get
a chance to excel, something happens to derail what once
had possibilities. The future looks bleak, life is passing you by
and there is little to live for.

President John F. Kennedy used to say that 'life's not
fair'. I do not know what made him say that. He had far
more advantages than most, but perhaps he was thinking
of people less fortunate than himself. However, what he

said is true. It is a wicked world.

Some think that being a Christian will eliminate all that is not good. But bad things happen to God's best, and often good things happen to the vile and venal. A Christian soon discovers that God allows injustice to happen to him or her, and such a person is then challenged over whether to complain or accept adversity with dignity.

Self-pity is not acceptable for the Christian, although we have all been guilty of this. If anything, I feel I have at times been the world's worst. Self-pity always feels right at the time, but it is almost always counter-productive when you vocalise it. Feel it if you must, but verbalising those feelings do not move the heart of God to come to your rescue. He is more likely to wait a while, and lead you step by step to grow up so that one day you can help others who have the same problem.

We now look at some classic examples of God's most famous servants who fell prey to self-pity. It may be somewhat consoling that you are in good company!

1. *Jacob, refusing to be comforted after believing that Joseph was dead.*
Yes, Jacob heads the list again. Isn't it comforting to know that even God's chief instruments made so many horrendous mistakes? I find his consoling, especially since I identify with Jacob so much!

What happened was this. The brothers sold Joseph to the Ishmaelites. Rather than tell Jacob what they had done, they took Joseph's coat of many colours and dipped it in blood – then laid it before Jacob. He took the bait, and asserted that Joseph was devoured by a wild animal. All his sons tried to comfort him, 'but he refused to be comforted . . . [and said] in mourning I will go down to the grave' (Gen. 37:28–35).

Self-pity is a sin against God. Jacob should have known better. True, the evidence was convincing. But the promises God gave to him, as well as those concerning his twelve sons – their posterity and prosperity, should have held him. He gave in to unbelief. God heard his words. The angels must have blushed. When we utter words of self-pity it exposes our unbelief and lack of confidence in God, not to mention that it is a poor testimony.

### 2. *Jacob, bearing a negative testimony to the Pharaoh.*

Jacob exhibited self-pity again when he was introduced to the Pharaoh years later. He had so much to praise God for. Joseph was alive! He is second only to the Pharaoh in Egypt! All his children and grandchildren have been preserved in this famine! All that God had promised him through dreams and visions was coming to pass! What goodness and mercy had been extended to Jacob.

And now Jacob has an opportunity to witness to the greatest king in the world. This was his moment. It does not come around to many people. What do you suppose Jacob said to the Pharaoh? He said, 'My years have been few and difficult, and they do not equal the years of the pilgrimage of my fathers' (Gen. 47:9). Never mind that Jacob was 130 years old! Here he is – in Egypt, having been restored to Joseph who was alive and well and Prime Minister – but still complaining. It was not the best testimony before the Pharaoh. He had every reason to be rejoicing! But no. He was still complaining.

How many of us would like to see a videotape of our words being played to the world when we had every reason under the sun to be thankful but complained instead?

3. *Elijah, claiming before God and men that he was the only prophet alive.*

Speaking to none other than God, Elijah said, 'I have been very zealous for the Lord God Almighty . . . I am the only one left, and now they are trying to kill me too' (1 Kings 19:14). First of all, Elijah was not the only prophet left and should have known better. Obadiah had taken a hundred prophets and hid them in a cave – and Elijah knew that (1 Kings 18:1–15). There were a good number of prophets around. But owing to persecution he was feeling sorry for himself. He took himself too seriously.

Self-pity often masks a feeling of self-importance and both spring from self-righteousness. Once before Elijah had stated publicly that he was the only prophet left – and uttered these thoughtless words in front of hundreds of the prophets of Baal. 'I am the only one of the Lord's prophets left,' he proclaimed (1 Kings 18:22). It shows he had completely dismissed those one hundred prophets that Obadiah had preserved. He thought he was a cut above them, that he was the only true prophet.

God is so patient with us when we utter foolish comments like that. Had God required sinless perfection before Elijah could be used, God would have interrupted the proceedings at Mount Carmel at once – and called the whole thing off. God could have thundered, 'NO, you are quite wrong' – and stopped the whole thing. But he let Elijah continue.

It was some time later that God said, as it were, 'Oh, by the way Elijah, you might like to know that I have reserved *seven thousand* who have not bowed down to Baal' (1 Kings 19:18). God patiently waited for the right time to deal with Elijah.

So too with us. When I think of my own self-importance and self-pity over the years – when I had so much to be thankful for and no right to be used – and yet God continued to use me, I blush.

4. *Job, and Jeremiah, cursing the day of their birth.*
We can sympathise with their plight. There is Job, not understanding what was going on when he lost everything, including his good health; and Jeremiah, being accused of treason because of his prophecies that Babylon would destroy Jerusalem.

There is often a reasonable explanation for a person giving in to self-pity. What Job suffered was extremely hard. But openly cursing the day of one's birth did not bless the Creator and was a terrible thing to utter (Job 3:1ff). He asked, 'Why did I not perish at birth, and die as I came from the womb?' (Job 3:11). As for the prophet Jeremiah, he said, 'Cursed be the day I was born!' (Jer. 20:14). Imagine a sovereign vessel who speaks for God talking like that!

The Holy Spirit did not lead either Jeremiah or Job to speak in this manner. The Holy Spirit, however, preserved their words for us to read. This is what they actually said, but that does not make it right merely because we know all ended well. We are not given these examples for us to imitate. We are given them, at least partly, for us to see that the best of God's children get extremely discouraged and say regrettable things.

5. *Jonah, when his prophecy to Nineveh was not vindicated.*
God told Jonah to go to Nineveh and prophesy against it (Jonah 1:2). He disobeyed and sought refuge in a ship sailing to Tarshish (Spain), but on this journey God sent such

a storm that the sailors (at Jonah's request) threw him overboard. But Jonah was swallowed up by a great fish and, while in the belly of the fish, repented and prayed that God might be gracious and let him please do the very thing he had rebelled against. God was gracious and gave Jonah a second chance, telling him to go to Nineveh (Jonah 3:1). He did, proclaiming, 'Forty more days and Nineveh will be overturned' (Jonah 3:4).

What Jonah feared most is exactly what happened. The people of Nineveh believed this word and repented – from the king down to the least person. Instead of destroying Nineveh, which Jonah was on record for promising, God showed mercy on them and 'did not bring upon them the destruction he had threatened' (Jonah 3:10).

Most preachers would have been thrilled from head to toe to see God move like that. But not Jonah. He was more interested in his prophecy being fulfilled – so he would be vindicated as a prophet – than he was in seeing the people of Nineveh spared.

Therefore, instead of rejoicing in a saved nation, 'Jonah was greatly displeased and became angry' (Jonah 4:1). It is surprising to many that a true man of God could have such a big ego and be so selfish. But Jonah 4:1–11 is an account of a person being overcome by self-pity. 'Now, O Lord, take away my life, for it is better for me to die than to live' (Jonah 4:3). In other words, Jonah would rather die than have the people of Nineveh live; he preferred their death to his embarrassment!

What is most extraordinary is the endless patience God had with Jonah. We might expect God to judge Jonah on the spot, but instead the Lord gently dealt with Jonah and brought him to a place of repentance. 'Have you any right to be angry?', God asked Jonah (Jonah 4:4).

Our vocalising self-pity, even when we are telling it to God, can bring us to such a distorted sense of right and wrong that we give God an invitation to judge us. He could do that. But as he was patient with Jonah, I know he has been patient with me. I identify with Jonah – all the way from his initial disobedience to his inexcusable self-pity. I have been Jonah more often than I want you to know. I would hate for you to eavesdrop on my words when my pride was threatened. You would be shocked. But God was patient with me, as he was with Jonah.

How do we know Jonah repented? Because, in telling the whole story of what happened, he gave God the last word (Jonah 4:10–11). When our words come back to haunt us, and show how low we can stoop in needing our self-esteem bolstered, we must thank God for his gracious dealings with us – then stop arguing with him. Give him the last word.

# 3

# Manipulating Providence

There is no wisdom, no insight, no plan that can succeed
against the Lord.

*Prov. 21:30*

God's providence is his overruling will in all our affairs.
He makes things happen. It is important to remember
this: *God has a plan* – a will of his own. He has already
decided what is good and right, what is best for us; he
works all things after the counsel of his own will
(Eph. 1:11). Only a fool will try to upstage what God has
already determined. But sometimes the best of God's
people do foolish things.

This often happens when we think he is not working fast
enough, or that he has forgotten us, or even that he did not
mean what he said. We tend to think sometimes that we can
step into his affairs and give him a little help! The truth is,

he doesn't want our help, and he certainly doesn't like it one bit if we fancy that we have more wisdom than he has.

### 1. *Joseph, when he tried to vindicate himself.*

When being falsely accused by Potiphar's wife (she accused him of trying to rape her), Joseph was put in prison. He was understandably angry and displeased. He had been betrayed by his brothers, and now this! He was a frustrated man. So when he saw a chance to get out of prison, he seized it. Prophesying to the king's cupbearer that he would get his job back in three days, Joseph inserted himself into the picture, like this: 'Remember me, and show me kindness; mention me to Pharaoh and get me out of this prison . . . I have done nothing to deserve being put in a dungeon' (Gen. 40:14–15). One truly sympathises with Joseph.

But God wasn't having it! God had big plans for him. Had God permitted the cupbearer to deliver this message to the Pharaoh before the right time, Joseph would have forfeited a brilliant future. Fortunately the cupbearer forgot to mention this to the Pharaoh. I personally think that God looked down into Joseph's cell and said, 'Oh Joseph, you should not have said that to the cupbearer. I think you will need a couple more years there.'

Love is not 'self-seeking' (1 Cor. 13:5). Had Joseph been utterly devoid of bitterness he would not have promoted himself like that. Had he already *totally* forgiven his brothers (and all others who hurt him) for what they did, I believe he would have been so filled with the Spirit of God that he would have known it was wrong to speak like that to the cupbearer. God wanted to promote Joseph without Joseph's manipulation. He wanted to show Joseph and Israel what can be done without any human help.

We all are tempted to nudge the arm of providence. We want to pull strings to get to the next level. Perhaps God permits this at times. But for the *big things* he has in mind for us, I myself have learned to let God do this. I would be afraid to promote myself lest I promote myself to the level of my incompetence! When we totally let God take charge, we will learn that he wants to do things for us in such a manner that we will always know it is what God did – and not us.

2. *The Israelites, claiming they could still enter Canaan when God swore that they couldn't.*

What happened was this. God sent twelve spies into the Promised Land to investigate the situation. Ten out of the twelve came back convinced that the Israelites dare not proceed into the land God had given Israel as an inheritance. 'We can't attack those people; they are stronger than we are,' said the ten spies. 'We seemed like grasshoppers in our own eyes, and we looked the same to them' (Num. 13:31, 33).

Caleb and Joshua, however, said in so many words, 'We can do it – let's go for it' (Num. 13:30). They were not given to unbelief like the majority.

But the majority ruled. It certainly was not the 'sanctified majority'. It was the unbelieving majority. The next night the people grumbled against Moses and wished they had died in Egypt. The whole assembly talked about stoning Joshua and Caleb. This is when God made a proposition to Moses to destroy the people and start all over again and Moses interceded on their behalf. Although God heard Moses' prayer – 'I have forgiven them, as you asked,' he nonetheless vowed that 'not one of the men who saw my glory and the miraculous signs I performed . . . will ever see the land' (Num. 14:20–23). This is when God swore in his wrath that they would not enter into his rest (see Heb. 3:11).

When God swears, it is 'all over' – period. There are no further conditions or qualifications – as in a general promise. A promise is usually given on a condition. But if God *swears*, there is nothing more that we can do. We cannot persuade him otherwise, no matter how many promises we make, no matter how hard we try. If he swears, that's it.

That is what happened with ancient Israel. God swore in his wrath that the people would not be allowed into Canaan – at all. And Moses told them that. And then, would you believe it, the people repented and said, 'We have sinned . . . we will go up . . .' Speaking like this is challenging God's wisdom and trying to overrule his providence. So Moses warned them, 'Do not go up, because the Lord is not with you. You will be defeated by your enemies.' But they utterly failed (Num. 14:44–45).

Our words cannot change God's mind when he has uttered an oath. There are these two unchangeable things – the promise and the oath (see Heb. 6:18). As long as there is a promise extended to us, we should take it with both hands. But when he declares his word in an oath, nothing will change his mind, no matter how long we talk or how loud we cry.

3. *Absalom, promoting himself to the kingship.*
After King David's sin (examined below), the beginnings of Nathan's prophecy 'the sword will never depart from your house' (2 Sam. 12:10) began to emerge. Probably the greatest grief David would suffer was from his own son Absalom. Absalom was angry with his father for refusing to see his face after he took vengeance upon his brother Amnon for

raping his sister (2 Sam. 13). He did something that eventually resulted in his forcing his father King David into exile.

Whereas God did not let Joseph's nudging the arm of providence succeed, he did allow Absalom to get his way – for a while.

Here is the way it started. He provided himself with a chariot and horses and with fifty men to run ahead of him. He would take a position near the city gate where everyone saw him. When people had their complaints to be placed before the king, Absalom would do things to endear himself to the people so they would be diverted from seeing the king. He flattered the people who came along and in an evil manner began to undermine the king with poisonous words.

Here was a typical conversation. Once he found out where a person was from Absalom would say, 'Look, your claims are valid and proper, but there is no representative of the king to hear you.' He would add, 'If only I were appointed judge in the land! Then everyone who has a complaint or case could come to me and I would see that he receives justice' (2 Sam. 15:3–5). Therefore, when people came into the city he would reach out his hand and kiss the person, bowing. 'Absalom behaved in this way towards all the Israelites who came to the king asking for justice, and so *he stole the hearts* of the men of Israel' (2 Sam. 15:6).

There have been not a few 'Number Two' men in various churches who have done this sort of thing. Not content to be Number Two – to which they had been called – they would undermine the leadership of the Senior Minister by flattering the people, making the true leader look detached from everybody and winning the hearts of the flock before the people realised what was happening. This is why every leader needs *loyalty* almost above anything else when looking for people to join the staff.

God had called David to kingship. But David had sinned and his kingdom was beginning to fall apart in places, not least in his own family.

Absalom succeeded. He tricked his father David into thinking he was going to worship the Lord in Hebron. Instead, Absalom had arranged people to shout – when the trumpets sounded – 'Absalom is king in Hebron.' The report came to King David, 'The hearts of the men of Israel are with Absalom' (2 Sam. 15:13). The result was that David was forced into exile. It was one of the saddest moments in his life.

David was eventually restored and Absalom was tragically killed, literally being hung by his own hair (2 Sam. 18:9–10). Even sadder, if that were possible, was the fact that Absalom built a monument to himself. He had erected it during his lifetime, thinking, 'I have no son to carry on the memory of my name.' So he named the pillar after himself (2 Sam. 18:18).

People who usurp the providence of God to advance themselves are doomed from the start. Although it would not have happened had David not sinned as he did, God still will punish those who foolishly promote themselves. The most they get is a monument to themselves, a stone that only reminds future generations of their utter folly.

Absalom's folly began with the tongue. He appeared to succeed for a while. He won the battle but lost the war.

# 4

# Trying to Prove Ourselves

You are the ones who justify yourselves in the eyes of men,
but God knows your hearts. What is highly valued among
men is detestable in God's sight.

*Luke 16:15*

My old friend Pete Cantrell often says, 'The greatest
freedom is having nothing to prove.' I think this is one of the
profoundest words I have ever heard. The person who needs
to prove how right or how strong he or she is, is one who
is not free. There is a struggle inside to make others think
they are right and strong. The truth is, if we really are right
and strong, we don't have to say anything! Freedom is being
experienced, therefore, when one has nothing to prove. He
or she does not need to justify themselves or make themselves look good. It is enough for people like that that *God
knows* (see John 5:44).

1. *Job, when he broke silence with his 'friends'*.
After Job lost his wealth and health, his three friends joined him. They came to comfort him. At first they saw him from a distance. They could hardly recognise him and began to weep openly. They tore their robes and sprinkled dust on their heads. They sat on the ground with him for seven days and nights. '*No one said a word* to him, because they saw how great his suffering was' (Job 2:13).

Who broke the silence? It was Job. This was a mistake. He was not required to say a word. If they were truly his friends, let *them* speak! But Job spoke first. Knowing traditional theology about sin and suffering, he almost certainly knew what they were thinking – that Job had sin in his life or this would not have happened. He felt a need to say something. He was not aware of a conscious sin against God, but knew what they were thinking in their hearts. So he wanted to say something that would at least imply how innocent he was. This was the first mistake – speaking at all. As my friend Pete Cantrell says, the greatest freedom is having nothing to prove. Job felt a need to break the silence.

The most natural feeling in the world is the urge to have your name cleared from blame. I know what it is to want vindication more than anything. One of the greatest lessons I have had to learn in fifty years of ministry is to 'let God do it'. Everything God does he does better than any of us. But if there is *anything* that God does best (if I may put it that way), it is the job of vindicating. He does it so brilliantly that, were *we* to interfere, he backs off. We therefore never know what might have been had he been free to do his job. When it comes to vindicating, he made it clear: it is his sole prerogative – 'it is mine to avenge; I will repay' (Rom. 12:19).

2. *Rehoboam, when he boasted of personal strength.*
The son of Solomon was implored to make the people's burdens lighter. He said he would think about it. He then replied with some of the saddest words in Holy Writ. I cringe every time I read this. 'My little finger is thicker than my father's waist. My father laid on you a heavy yoke; I will make it even heavier' (1 Kings 12:10–11).

It is small men who talk like this. They have a need to prove themselves and show how strong, how manly, how secure they are. Rehoboam's decision was a turning point in the ancient history of Israel. He was afraid of being seen as less than strong. He knew how highly respected his father was. He thought he would get more respect by showing what a tyrant is like. He lost – everybody lost.

Paul said that Jesus was crucified in 'weakness' (2 Cor. 13:4) – which in fact showed our Lord's greatest strength. He had the power to call ten thousand angels to come down and deliver him. He who raised the dead and walked on water could have come down from the cross the moment he was challenged to do so. But no. He let them do what they did. He lost the battle in order to win the war – our redemption.

When we have a need to show how strong we are I think of Shakespeare's famous line, 'Methinks the lady doth protest too much.' The greatest strength is having the confidence to prove nothing at the time in order that God will show his glory and power in his time.

3. *The Pharisee in the temple, trying to justify himself.*
Jesus gave one of his best-known parables, describing a tax collector and a Pharisee. The Pharisee said, 'God, I thank you that I am not like other men – robbers, evildoers, adul-

terers – or even like this tax collector. I fast twice a week and give a tenth of all I get' (Luke 18:10–12). Jesus gave this parable to those who were 'confident of their own righteousness'. The funny thing is, they needed to prove themselves, like the Pharisee – 'I am not like others.' Shakespeare said that 'comparisons are odious', but the worst kind of comparison is when you think you are a cut above others. And when you have a need to say something that makes yourself look good in the light of a person who seems so bad by comparison, it is because you are not free. And in the case of the Pharisee, not justified before God.

It was the tax collector, however, who would not even look up to heaven but beat his breast and said, 'God, have mercy on me, a sinner.' According to Jesus, it was the tax collector, not the Pharisee, who was justified before God (Luke 18:13–14).

When you are justified before God, you are free. Seeking to be justified, or vindicated, before people is a crippling, endless and counter-productive enterprise; you are never at peace. No freedom. But when you know that *God himself* declares you righteous, you are free and have no need to get your satisfaction from comparing yourselves with others.

The heart of the gospel is at stake here. What justifies us before God – our good works? Or is it our confession to God that we are sinners? Answer: we are justified when we do not try to prove ourselves before God but lean on his mercy. The way a person is converted is to ask God for mercy. Not only that; in this very parable the Greek behind the word 'mercy' really means 'God, be propitiated for me.' The Greek word is *hilaskomai* – a word that corresponds to 'mercy seat', the place in the holy of holies where the blood made atonement for sins. Jesus used a word that combined not only mercy but the need for sacrifice of blood. This is what the tax collector was pleading on his behalf – not his works.

When we are trusting our works, there will always be a need to try to prove ourselves – by words. The greatest freedom is having nothing to prove. This freedom comes when we put all our 'eggs into one basket', namely, the death of Jesus on the cross. That brings freedom because this alone is what justifies us before God.

# 5

# Speaking out of Fear

Do not be anxious about anything.

*Phil. 4:6*

Speaking out of fear always leads to evil (Ps. 37:8). God has not given us a spirit of fear (2 Tim. 1:7). Perfect love casts out fear (1 John 4:18). When we fear – and speak at the same time – what we say will come out wrong and may get us into serious trouble.

1. *Abraham, telling people that his wife was his sister.*
Abraham journeyed to Egypt and, knowing how beautiful his wife Sarah was, ordered her to say that she was his sister – so both of them would be spared. Abraham feared that someone would kill him in order to have her. So she did what he commanded.

It worked for a while. She was taken into Pharaoh's palace, where she was safe, while Abraham prospered. But

God stepped in. The Lord inflicted serious diseases on Pharaoh and his household because of Sarah. Pharaoh somehow knew that God had caused these diseases and knew that Sarah was Abraham's wife. 'Why didn't you tell me she was your wife?' (Gen. 12:18). Mercifully Abraham and Sarah were spared. They would never know what God himself might have done had they trusted him. Years later Isaac made the same mistake, repeating the error of his father (Gen. 26:7–22).

Speaking out of fear comes from assuming that God is not going to look after us – so we speak in unbelief. It is the folly of self-protection. The truth is, God stepped in for both Abraham and Isaac. He will for us too. But when we give in to unbelief and speak – thinking we are justifiably protecting ourselves – our sin has a way of backfiring on us.

*2. Jacob, fearing his reunion with his brother Esau.*

Jacob had not seen his brother in years. The last word Jacob had about Esau was that Esau was hell-bent on getting vengeance upon him for stealing Esau's birthright (Gen. 27:42–44). Jacob had lived in mortal fear all these years, knowing they would sooner or later meet up. The time had come. Jacob received the message: Esau 'is coming to meet you, and four hundred men are with him' (Gen. 32:6). This news terrified Jacob. He cried to God, 'Save me, I pray, from the hand of my brother Esau, for I am afraid he will come and attack me, and also the mothers [Rachael and Leah] with their children' (Gen. 32:11).

Jacob divided the people who were with him into two groups. He commanded his servant to speak to Esau and tell him that all the animals present were to be a gift to Esau. Fearing for his life, Jacob thought that bribing Esau with hundreds of goats, camels, donkeys and cows would pacify him (Gen. 32:14–18).

It was at that time Jacob experienced one of his greatest visitations from God – when he wrestled with the Angel who changed his name to Israel (Gen. 32:22–28). One would have thought this was all Jacob needed. Surely such an experience would increase his faith and take away all fear! But no. He was still filled with anxiety. He divided the children in such a manner that showed he was still scared nearly to death (Gen. 33:1–2).

But when they actually met each other it was a most happy moment. They hugged each other and wept. Esau was grateful for the offer of the gifts but said, 'I already have plenty, my brother. Keep what you have for yourself' (Gen. 33:9), but eventually he accepted the gift.

But there is more. Whereas Esau wanted to have more fellowship with his brother, Jacob in panic made up a story that got him away from Esau as soon as possible, hoping never to see him again. All Jacob did with Esau was to feign words of praise, gratitude and devotion, and promised to meet up shortly. The truth is, Jacob wanted out of there – and took off immediately (Gen. 33:12–17).

Jacob in fact lost the victory that should have been his. Esau turned out to be the gracious man. Jacob, God's chosen vessel, disgraced himself before God and the angels by his fear over nothing. 'Do not fret – it only leads to evil' (Ps. 37:8).

3. *Moses, feeling inadequate for the task God called him to.*
It was such an honour to be called to deliver the people of God from Pharaoh's bondage. Moses may well have appreciated this, but all he did was to argue back. 'O Lord, I

have never been eloquent . . . I am slow of speech and tongue . . . Please send someone else to do it.' God did not like that. 'The Lord's anger burned against Moses', but he offered to let Aaron assist him (Exod. 4:9–17).

The fact that God was displeased with Moses' response indicates that the role of Aaron was Plan B. We will never know what might have occurred in ancient Israel had Moses not given in to fear. What we do know is that Aaron turned out to be a real problem again and again, co-operating with the rebellion that surfaced with the Israelites.

Many people think that it is modest and noble to avoid Christian service due to a feeling of inadequacy. But when it is sheer unbelief, the Holy Spirit is quenched. What God calls us to do he enables us to do. St Augustine prayed, 'Command what Thou wilt, and give what Thou commandest.' When we say 'No' to the calling of God, whatever our reason, our tongue will witness against us.

We may think that our words do not matter if only God hears us. But he is the most important witness of all! We should care most of all what he thinks about our reaction to his word.

# 6

# Losing your Temper

A fool gives full vent to his anger, but a wise man keeps himself under control.

*Prov. 29:11*

Speaking personally, I fear this is where I have sinned the most over the years. I have shouted at my wife and my children more often than I dare think about. I know that the Deacons at Westminster Chapel feared my temper, certainly in earlier days there – some of them bravely told me so. I know what it is to speak sharply to a slow waitress in a restaurant, an incompetent clerk in a store or to people moving too slowly in the queue at a supermarket. I have been impatient with people in the Vestry at Westminster Chapel – right after preaching a good sermon! Instead of demonstrating gentleness I would look at my watch and wonder how long these people were going to keep asking inane questions. Undoubtedly one of my greatest weaknesses has been that I do not 'suffer fools gladly'.

The man who controls his temper is greater than a powerful warrior 'who takes a city' (Prov. 16:32). 'Wisdom makes one wise man more powerful than ten rulers in a city' (Eccles. 7:19). Remember that wisdom is knowing what to say next — and what not to say. It is no small consolation to know that God does not give up easily on us and he has graciously shown me that he is not finished with me yet.

There is a thin line sometimes between righteous anger and losing your temper. The difference is that when it is righteous anger you do not lose control. Are there biblical examples of losing one's temper?

1. *Moses, the manner in which he addressed the people for their grumbling.*
They longed to be back in Egypt — and blamed Moses for everything they didn't like, including there being no water to drink. Moses was certainly put on the spot. He went into the Tent of Meeting and fell face down and the glory of the Lord appeared. Then the Lord explicitly told Moses to '*speak to that rock* before their eyes and it will pour out its water'. But instead of speaking to the rock — which was Christ (1 Cor. 10:3) — he spoke to *them*. He scolded them, 'Listen, you rebels, must *we* bring you water out of this rock?' He had taken things personally despite God's gracious word and felt challenged to prove his leadership. Instead of speaking to the rock he verbally attacked the people. He then struck the rock twice with his staff. Although water gushed out, Moses had a lot to answer for. God immediately said to him, 'Because you did not trust in me enough to honour me as holy in the sight of the Israelites, you will not bring this community into the land I give them' (Num. 20:3–12).

What happened was this. He took their criticism personally and lost control by turning on them rather than simply speaking to the rock. 'Because they provoked his spirit, so that he spake unadvisedly with his lips' (Ps. 106:33, KJV). 'Rash words came from Moses' lips' (NIV).

Moses was probably the greatest leader of people in world history. But he was not perfect. The people wore him down; he could take it no more. Instead of speaking to the rock – which would have defied a natural explanation so that God would get all the glory for the water that gushed out, he struck it – making it something he did. I think that his rash words with the people may have caused the anointing on him to lift – which is why he did not carry through with the Lord's command.

## 2. *Paul, before the Sanhedrin.*

As Paul began to testify, the high priest ordered those near Paul to strike him on the mouth. Paul retorted, 'God will strike you, you whitewashed wall! You sit there to judge me according to the law, yet you yourself violate the law by commanding that I be struck!' Those near Paul said, 'You dare to insult God's high priest?' Then Paul mellowed, 'I did not realise that he was the high priest; for it is written: "Do not speak evil about the ruler of your people"' (Acts 23:1–5).

I am aware that many interpreters of this account would find no fault in Paul's behaviour. I disagree with them. To be sure, Paul is my greatest hero. But he wasn't perfect. Luke shows that he was clearly seen by those around him as having insulted the high priest. What he said, even if it had not been to the high priest, is not a display of meekness. Paul implicitly admits this. It was not his finest hour. But from that point on he was brilliant; the anointing clearly did not lift from him. I am sure that he repented for calling the man in charge (even if he did not know it was the high priest) a 'whitewashed wall'. I know that I have done this sort of thing, then I lowered my voice and quietly repented before the Lord in order to have clear thinking from then on.

# 7

# Lust

Each one is tempted when, by his own evil desire, he is dragged away and enticed.

*Js 1:14*

Sexual sin, whether it be adultery or pre-marital sex, usually begins with *words*. A person may be inwardly tempted. But once a word is uttered that registers what is going on inside, all hell can break loose. As long as one kept quiet about it, the devil was kept at bay. But once either the man or the woman lets it be known that there is a sexual attraction going on, it is like a spark igniting a forest fire. The tongue is 'a fire', and James was not merely referring to people losing their temper (Js 3:6).

1. *David, sending for Bathsheba and getting her to sleep with him.* At the very height of his kingship, when David was enjoying every success imaginable – nothing going wrong and

everything going right – he did something that was so very, very foolish. Some think he was bored with success. But it is apparent that he should have carried through with what kings did at a time like that – going to war (2 Sam. 11:1). But he didn't. He let others do it. He stayed behind. What we know is, David got up from an afternoon nap and noticed from his balcony a woman bathing. Some want to blame her for making herself available, but this is sheer speculation. The culprit was King David. If only he had turned away the moment he saw her.

But no. He spoke. His tongue got him into more trouble than he would ever imagine. One could not blame him if he was attracted to a woman washing herself, as the KJV put it. And the Bible even makes a point by saying she was 'very beautiful' (2 Sam. 11:2), as if to make one sympathise somewhat with David. Indeed, he could have been forgiven for thinking, 'Wow, that is one beautiful woman.' After all, men are normally aroused by sight. But he gave in. He should have done the responsible and mature thing – to turn away from looking at her immediately, and get on with being the good king that he was. Until then.

But, sadly, he spoke, ordering someone on his staff to get him information that was none of his business. He said something like, 'Find out who that beautiful woman is.' It was a fatal attraction. What followed – moments later, days later, years and years later – could have been avoided but for the tongue. It is so often what gets us into trouble. Having ordered someone to find out who she was, the reply came: she is a married woman, her name is Bathsheba, and her husband is Uriah the Hittite and is even one of your soldiers in the battle (2 Sam. 11:1–3).

The king could not have had a greater warning than that.

It left him utterly without excuse. But David was not content with the information that she was a married woman. He sent for her to come to his residence.

She came to him, he slept with her and she returned home. What both of them may have thought would be merely a one-off afternoon affair ended in one of the greatest tragedies described in the Old Testament. She sent word back a few weeks later: 'I'm pregnant.' This was certainly not good news. But David had what seemed to be an easy solution. He sent for Uriah, pretended to want information about how the battle was going and then told him to have a few days off and spend time with Bathsheba his wife. This seemed to him a benign way to cover his sin. But Uriah was an honourable man – having what some might call an overly scrupulous conscience. He refused to sleep with his wife, knowing that his fellows soldiers were risking their lives in the battle. David even ate and drank with him, trying to get him drunk. Uriah still would not see his wife.

The unthinkable followed. King David instructed his general Joab to place Uriah in the front of the battle so Uriah would be mortally wounded. It happened precisely that way. To cover his sin of adultery David thus resorted to murder (2 Sam. 11:4–17).

It is often said that whereas men are sexually aroused by sight, women are aroused by tender *words*, sometimes flattery (although it can happen the other way around too). The point is, whatever non-verbal exchange might be taking place – by communication through the eyes, for example – it is when one *speaks*, and he or she reveals desire for the other person, that sexual excitement is often caught by that other person and the passion cannot often be controlled.

But someone will say, 'If one lusts – and Jesus calls this adultery in the heart – one might as well carry out the physical act.' Wrong. That's the devil talking. Jesus was trying to teach the Pharisees a lesson about the nature of sin (Matt. 5:27–30). The physical act of adultery is infinitely worse than the lust of the heart. In any case, a good number of competent evangelical scholars believe that the Greek shows that what was adultery in the heart was *trying to create lust in the other*. The sin was causing the other to lust, whether by words from the man or provocative dress by the woman. But though this is adultery in the heart and needs to be repented of, it is the physical act of adultery that brings disaster, the heartache, the pain, the regret.

Billy Graham recently said that it seems the devil gets seventy-five per cent of God's best servants through sexual temptation. It is inflamed with words – flattery, flirting and seducing through conversation.

If you are reading these lines, man or woman, and you are involved – even potentially – in an affair, I would come to you right now and say to you, STOP IT – break it off. Now. The day will come, it will surely come, when you would give a thousand worlds if you could turn the clock back to this very moment.

2. *Samson, revealing his secret to Delilah.*
Samson was famous for his tremendous strength. I doubt any human being before or since had strength like he did. But it did not have a natural explanation; it was solely by the Holy Spirit. On one occasion, for example, 'The Spirit of the Lord came upon him in power so that he tore the lion apart with his bare hands as he might have torn a young goat' (Judg. 14:6). On another occasion he caught 300 foxes

and tied them tail to tail in pairs, fastened a torch to every pair of tails, lit the torches and let the foxes loose in certain fields of the Philistines – which destroyed their crop (Judg. 15:5). He once struck down 1,000 men with a jawbone of a donkey (Judg. 15:15).

The Philistines were determined to find out the *secret* of Samson's strength. Their intelligence revealed that Samson's weakness was, simply, women. He even frequented prostitutes and the word spread (Judg. 16:1–2).

By the way, what is your weakness? We all have them. It is sometimes referred to as one's 'besetting sin', or 'the sin that so easily entangles' (Heb. 12:1). You can be sure that Satan has a computer printout of your DNA, your lifestyle, your habits and your weaknesses. He will work overtime through those who can get to you and tempt you in the area of your weakness. Be aware of this. 'Clothe yourselves with the Lord Jesus Christ, and do not think about how to gratify the desires of the sinful nature' or, as it is put in the KJV, 'make not provision for the flesh, to fulfil the lusts thereof' (Rom. 13:14).

In the meantime Samson fell in love with a woman whose name was Delilah. The rulers of the Philistines asked her to see if she could lure him into revealing the secret of his great strength. They promised her money if she would comply. She did. She pressed him day after day to reveal the secret of his strength. He kept making up stories, refusing to tell her.

But finally, after she nagged him 'day after day until he was tired to death', he gave in. He told her everything. 'No razor has ever been used on my head . . . if my head were shaved, my strength would leave me, and I would become as weak as any other man' (Judg. 16:17). Shortly after that, while he was asleep on her lap, she arranged to have his hair cut. His strength left him. When the Philistines seized him they gouged out his eyes and took him down to Gaza. Binding him with bronze shackles, they put him in prison. It would not have happened had he been able to control his tongue.

What if you had an unusual anointing – and there was a secret to it? It is between you and God. Would you be able to keep quiet about it? Would you cave in and reveal the secret under pressure? It could be that your particular weakness is not sexual temptation but, say, needing the admiration of certain people. Would you value the anointing more than having anybody know the secret to it? The psalmist said that the Lord 'confides' in those who fear him. The KJV says the 'secret of the Lord' is with them that fear him (Ps. 25:14). Most people cannot keep secrets. I have long felt that God would do far more for us if we could keep quiet about it. God may be pleased to give you an unusual and extraordinary anointing – on the condition that you were to keep quiet about it.

God was merciful to Samson in the end. While in prison his hair began to grow. When they brought him into a large place to make fun of him, he asked to be put where he could feel the pillars that supported the temple. Three thousand were present. Samson prayed, 'O Sovereign Lord, remember me, O God, please strengthen me just once more, and let me with one blow get revenge on the Philistines for my two eyes'. Bracing himself against the pillars in which the temple stood he cried out 'Let me die with the Philistines!' and the temple came down on all the rulers and all the people in it. 'Thus he killed more people when he died than while he lived' (Judg. 16:30).

Samson had a brief but strategic restoration in the end –
at the very last. 'All's well that ends well,' said Shakespeare.
And Samson's example holds out hope for those who have
fallen and who may feel there is no chance of being used
again. One of the next books I write will deal with this and
will show how God does take fallen heroes and bring them
back to repentance. It could therefore be said of Samson,
that when the future seemed hopeless, God wasn't finished
with him yet.

# Part Two
# Success in Controlling the Tongue

True instruction was in his mouth and nothing false was found on his lips. He walked with me in peace and uprightness, and turned many from sin.

*Mal. 2:6*

These words in Malachi 2:6 describe the kind of life God required for priests in the Old Testament. These words are found on the tombstone of Jonathan Edwards (1703–1758), the man God sovereignly used in the Great Awakening in New England and the greatest theologian in American history. I would wish more than anything that God himself might make this claim about me after I am gone. Every minister should want these words to describe him or her.

It will be recalled that James says, 'If anyone is never at fault in what he says, he is a perfect man' (Js 3:2). And yet enjoying a measure of success in controlling the tongue on occasion does not mean you are perfect! I can assure you that you have not 'arrived' – even if you go three days without an unguarded comment – neither is the problem of controlling the tongue now behind you. Tongue control is only a temporary grace – given one day at a time; and hour by hour even when you are having a good day.

I don't mean to be discouraging. But a New Testament doctrine of sanctification is needed here. We need both a scriptural and a realistic understanding of biblical holiness. Any teaching which purports that you, before you get to Heaven, can be totally sanctified – soul, spirit, body *and tongue* – is unbiblical and misleading. People who are taught such a notion often get frustrated, even demoralised, by their attempts to maintain perfection.

I should know. I was brought up in a denomination that emphasised 'entire sanctification' (based upon 1 Thess. 5:23), stressing in particular what was known as 'two works of grace' – being 'saved' (the first work) and 'sanctified' (the second work). The second work was said to have eradicated the sinful, carnal nature. Many theologians in that denomination came to alter that understanding, it is only fair to say. But I know what I myself was taught. I would go to the 'altar' again and again to get the 'second blessing' so that I did not lose my temper ever again – and finally experience control of the tongue. I never got it. I never met anybody who did! This would include my godly parents. They were as 'good as they come', but they did not have what their church leaders told them they had. They might make excuses for their 'faults', 'errors', 'mistakes' – they would never ever call them *sin*. They were sincere, but misguided.

This book is not a treatise on the New Testament doctrine of sanctification. I have dealt with this in other books (you might take a look at my *Understanding Theology*). But let me summarise what the Bible teaches about sanctification. I would define it as *the process by which we become more and more like Jesus*. But we never become totally pure and sinless in this life. However, we can certainly make progress. It is a daily exercise to fight the flesh and to resist temptation – whether that temptation refers to pride, sex, fear or tongue control.

In a word: we never become sinlessly perfect in this life. God saves sinless perfection for glorification – when we are in Heaven. In the meantime we must daily mortify the deeds of the body, fighting against the world, the flesh and the devil (Rom. 6:11–14). This we can certainly do because we are under grace. We must not go on in wilful sinning that grace may abound (Rom. 6:1), but we are still loaded with imperfections and the proneness to come short of God's glory (Rom. 3:23). This is why we need the daily cleansing of Christ's blood (1 John 1:7). We have the Holy Spirit, moreover, to resist temptation and to grow in grace, thus manifesting the fruits of the Spirit in ever-increasing measure (Gal. 5:22–23).

Never being at fault in what one *says*, then, means perfection. James is obviously not expecting that of any Christian, as the following verses (examined below), show. So the tongue is something you must live with, work with, get victory over – little by little – every day. But one day at a time! It is terrific when you have a good day. It is very encouraging. But if you have had a good day, I lovingly caution you: wait until tomorrow!

I know what it is sometimes to preach well, to come down from the pulpit with an inner confidence and I say to myself, 'Well, at last I have learned how to preach.' But when I feel like that for very long, here is what happens – nearly every time: I do so poorly the next time I am in the pulpit that I leave saying, 'If that is the best I can do I should get out of the ministry.' So if you have a good day with tongue control, thank God for it; but don't be deluded that you have mastered the art of tongue control; you just might be a miserable failure the next day.

The truth is, however, that we can improve. We do get better at it. The reward is worth the effort, I promise you. That is why I write this book! There is hope for us all! Success in controlling the tongue is something that we must pray for all the time. This book is designed to help.

This is a word that can indeed also apply to a preacher or a writer. We must learn to waste no words – whether in the pulpit or with the pen. I don't mean that I have tips on how to preach or write, but tongue control in our personal lives should have the effect of helping us to know when to stop preaching or writing. Some preachers seem never to know when to stop – and drive their hearers mad. I would rather quit when the congregation is wanting me to keep on preaching than for them to say to themselves at the end of the sermon, 'I'm certainly glad that's over.' So in writing. I pray the Holy Spirit will enable me to say all I need to say in this very book – and to stop at the right time.

But this book is about everyday conversation. It is about showing self-restraint with the number of words when you are in conversation (learning not to tire people out) but also about making the right choice of words – with friends, relatives, spouses, fellow Christians and people we run into all the time. 'A man of knowledge uses words with restraint, and a man of understanding is even-tempered' (Prov. 17:27). I want this book to be a contribution to your knowledge – that it will make a definite, a life-changing, impact on your personal life.

We will now look at examples of those who had success in controlling the tongue. These will often include those very people already seen in this book as having failed! Only Jesus – our ultimate example – was perfect. But God is gracious and gives us moments and occasions when we get it right.

# 8

# Climbing Down

The first to present his case seems right, till another come
forward and questions him.

*Prov. 18:17*

It is not easy to admit that you have been wrong. Nothing
challenges our big egos like being faced with the evidence
that says, plainly, you were wrong! And then you have to
climb down.

I have had to face this many times. I die a thousand deaths
before I give in, you can be sure. I will hold out until the
end – hoping against hope that *I was not wrong*!

The problem is often this. We may have taken a stand on
a situation. People disagree with us. It could be a decision
about a person and what they did; it could be a theological
point of view; it could be about a job; a choice of a church,
the value of a particular minister; directions in traffic; who
should be elected to political office; it might be the choice

of where to spend a vacation. The list is endless.

I know of well-known church leaders – not to mention political leaders – who would not change their position simply because they put their point of view in print – or stated something publicly. We back ourselves into a corner and become defensive. It hurts to admit you got it wrong when a lot of people know what you said or did.

I had to do this publicly with the 'Toronto blessing'. When I first heard that strange things were happening at Holy Trinity, Brompton, a prominent Anglican church in London, I had little difficulty dismissing it all as the latest fad in one stroke – people being prayed for, falling on the floor and laughing their heads off. Surely this could not be God, I said. For one thing, I did not *want* it to be of God (that would be threatening indeed). For I find that sort of thing highly offensive. For another thing, if it really were of God it would have come to Westminster Chapel first! After all, we (not them) had borne the heat of the day; we had our prayer meetings, we were witnessing faithfully on the streets of Westminster; I had put my reputation on the line again and again. God would bless us before he would bless the Church of England (which I regarded as largely apostate). It would be a betrayal should God bless an upper-middle-class Anglican church with their posh, Etonian accents!

Immediately after I heard about these bizarre things taking place at Holy Trinity I made a public statement about it from the pulpit at Westminster Chapel. I cautioned my people against this, although I did admit that church history indicates that God can do some awfully strange things to confound the sophisticated. So I took my stand.

I have described the process elsewhere (see *In Pursuit of His Glory* and *The Anointing*), so I will simply say here that, some weeks later, I stood in the same pulpit at Westminster Chapel and said 'I was wrong' – that what was going on at Holy Trinity was indeed of God and I also encouraged people to go there and get prayed for. By the way, I have never been sorry I climbed down; it turned out to be one of the most important decisions I took in my twenty-five years at Westminster Chapel.

It feels good to admit you were wrong! Yes, it hurts our pride. And there will certainly be those who question your judgement and will always be suspicious of you for the rest of your life. But the inner peace that comes from the Holy Spirit compensates a thousand times over for the embarrassment your 'climb down' brought about.

There were people in the Bible who had to climb down too.

1. *Samuel, who thought that Eliab would be God's choice to be the next king.*
He had come to the house of Jesse to anoint the next king. He looked at Eliab, Jesse's first-born. In ancient Israel the first-born son always received double the inheritance. It was natural for Samuel to think that Eliab was the one. He even said so. 'He looked on Eliab, and said, Surely the Lord's anointed is before him' (1 Sam. 16:6, KJV). When a prophet with the stature of a Samuel makes an utterance like that, imagine how thrilled and humbled both Eliab and Jesse were. But Samuel had jumped the gun.

God stepped in and said to Samuel, 'Do not consider his appearance or his height, for I have rejected him. The Lord does not look at the things man looks at. Man looks at the outward appearance, but the Lord looks at the heart' (1 Sam. 16:7). As I say in *The Anointing*, Samuel was a type of 'today's man' and to be on the cutting edge of what God is going to do in our own generation, we must be in continual readiness to admit our mistakes and say so when, after all, we have got it wrong. A prophet has to do this; a theologian has to do this; a church leader has to do this. A husband has to do this with his wife and family. A boss has to do this in the office. A political leader has to do this before a nation – if he has the humility to do so.

Jonathan Edwards taught us that the task of every generation is to discover in which direction the Sovereign Redeemer is moving, then move in that direction. I, for one, do not want to miss what direction God is moving in. This means I must continually swallow my pride and be willing to correct past mistakes and failures – however great the stigma. Otherwise any anointing I have will lift from me. It is my greatest fear that the anointing would be taken from me and I would become yesterday's man.

Samuel went through all the sons of Jesse, seven of them, and was about to give up! 'Are these all the sons you have?' he asked. Jesse admitted there was one more son – young David, tending the sheep – but Jesse for some reason did not seem very keen to waste time with him. But Samuel said, 'Send for him; we will not sit down until he arrives.' When David came in the Lord said, 'Rise and anoint him; he is the one' (1 Sam. 16:12). God frequently chooses sovereign vessels that you and I would overlook – all because of our prejudices. God loves to surprise us and especially select someone that we, who are so traditional, erudite and cultured, will want to reject.

If you and I are going to be God's instruments in our time we must be willing to climb down, admit to our errors, throw our reputations to the wind and worship God. The anointing we get in return is worth it all.

## 2. *Nathan the prophet, having encouraged David to get on with his dream to build a temple.*

We saw earlier that the prophet Samuel had to climb down from a word he gave to Jesse. Another prophet, Nathan, had the trust of King David. David had conquered Jerusalem, brought the ark there, won every war he fought, and now was looking for more to do. He wanted to build a temple for the Lord.

He called in Nathan the prophet. 'Here I am, living in a palace of cedar, while the ark of God remains in a tent.' Nathan hastily said to David, 'Whatever you have in mind, go ahead and do it, for the Lord is with you' (2 Sam. 7:1–3). When a man with enormous prophetic stature talks like that, you take it seriously! God was certainly with David, there was no doubt about that; Nathan therefore apparently felt as safe as could be in telling him to get on with whatever was on his heart.

But before Nathan was permitted to go to sleep, on that very same night, the Lord came to him and told him, in so many words, to climb down from what he had said to King David (2 Sam. 7:4–16). Nathan had the task of reporting the revelation – that God said 'No, David, you can't build the temple after all,' and David accepted Nathan's latest word.

It smacks of transparent integrity when a person known to have a prophetic gift has the honesty and courage to say, 'Sorry, I got it wrong.' Few do this, I fear. They are afraid they will lose their authority if they take back what they said. So people like this make a choice: take back what you said or lose your anointing. That should be an easy decision, but apparently not for some. The truth is, prophets are people. Not every word that comes from their lips is inspired by the Holy Spirit. But sometimes their followers think otherwise, and sometimes a prophetic person seems to want people to hang on to their every word.

Nathan must have been one of the greatest prophets of all time. He was a man of unusual prophetic gifting but also of tremendous courage. What follows is an example of how this same Nathan had to confront David with some of the most fearful words ever given from a prophet to a man in authority.

3. *David, having been so self-righteous about the person described in Nathan's parable.*

We have already seen David's sin and attempted cover-up by having Uriah killed. Some time later God sent Nathan the prophet to David with a parable, describing how a rich man, instead of taking one of his own sheep or cattle to provide a meal, had taken instead the only ewe lamb that belonged to a poor man. David went ballistic. He 'burned with anger' and vowed, 'As surely as the Lord lives, the man who did this deserves to die! He must pay for that lamb four times over, because he did such a thing and had no pity' (2 Sam. 12:1–6).

Nathan replied: 'You are the man!' and commenced to describe to David what David had done (and thought he had got away with) in sleeping with Bathsheba and striking down Uriah. He added, 'The sword shall never depart from your house, because you despised me and took the wife of Uriah the Hittite to be your own' (2 Sam. 12:10).

Self-righteousness is an exceedingly difficult sin to see in ourselves. Part of our inherited depravity from Adam is self-love and pride. We are quick to judge others, slow to see the equivalent sin in ourselves. Who would have thought a sin like adultery and murder would need a parable to make a person see his wrong! But sometimes the most heinous sins have a way of camouflaging our perception, and causing us to miss seeing the most obvious maladies we have. That was David.

The only man in the Bible called a man 'after God's own heart' (see 1 Sam. 13:14; Acts 13:22) was guilty of one of the most shameful sins and crimes in ancient Israelite history. But one of the proofs that he was indeed a man after God's own heart was in his reaction to Nathan.

David climbed down. No defensiveness. No justification for what he did. He owned everything on the spot: 'I have sinned against the Lord' (2 Sam. 12:13). He meant it and took to heart every word Nathan continued to say. It makes one think of a well-known TV evangelist who, when found out, said before the world, 'I have sinned' – but immediately dug in his heals when his denominational authorities gave him instructions as to the way forward – and refused counsel. This is the way one becomes yesterday's man or woman.

God wasn't finished with David yet. True, there was a blight on his life and he was under a cloud that lasted a long time. But he continued to write psalms, he was still used by the Lord. Let no one think that sin, however great, necessarily finishes you off. Enter into Psalm 51 and pray with David, admitting your guilt and asking for mercy; and know too the hope he had: 'Then I will teach transgressors your ways, and sinners will turn back to you' (Ps. 51:13). Or as it is put in Psalm 130:4: 'But with you there is forgiveness; therefore you are feared.'

We have a big God – who has provided a sacrifice for our sins in his Son Jesus Christ. 'If we confess our sins, he is faithful and just and will forgive us our sins and purify us from all unrighteousness' (1 John 1:9). God has been appeased by the blood of his Son and all we need do is to confess our sins to God, turn from them and move on.

Who is a God like you, who pardons sin and forgives the transgression of the remnant of his inheritance? You do not stay angry forever but delight to show mercy.

Mic. 7:18

4. *Naaman, having been offended by Elisha's instructions on how to be healed.*
Naaman, an army general under the king of Aram, was a leper. He was told that if he could get to Elisha the prophet he would be healed. It took a lot of faith and humility for a man like this to come over into Israel – having also to clear this with the king of Israel – and then ask to be healed by someone he did not know. The link was a young girl from Israel who was a servant to the general's wife. She kept saying to her mistress, 'If only my master would see the prophet who is in Samaria! He would cure him of his leprosy' (2 Kings 5:3).

Naaman eventually found his way to Elisha's house. But Elisha did not even come out to greet Naaman. A general is not used to being treated like that. This was almost certainly a blow to his pride. But not only did the prophet Elisha not come out to meet Naaman, he merely sent a messenger to say to the general, 'Go, wash yourself seven times in the Jordan, and your flesh will be restored and you will be cleansed' (2 Kings 5:10).

Naaman was indignant. How dare Elisha treat him like that! As for the word the messenger actually sent, it was adding insult to injury. Wash seven times in the River Jordan! This must be some sort of a joke. So he refused to comply. He left in a rage. But he did explain how nothing went according to his expectation. 'I thought that he would surely come out to me and stand and call on the name of the Lord his God, wave his hand over the spot and cure me of my leprosy.' Even though Naaman was a Syrian, knowing virtually nothing of the ways of the God of Israel, he still thought he knew how the famous prophet would perform. He was not prepared to be treated in this manner. Nothing made sense. Not only that, if he was to wash in a river, 'Are not Abana and Pharpar, the rivers of Damascus, better than any of the waters of Israel? Couldn't I wash in them and be cleansed?'

God not only seems to delight in offending the sophisticated by the vessel he chooses but by the *manner of ministry* as well. It certainly made perfect sense for Naaman to be cleansed by the rivers at home. Why ever not?

This is the kind of question people ask, 'Why do I have to go to Toronto to be blessed?' 'Why do I have to be prayed for by this or that person – won't my own minister do as well?' 'Why do I have to go to this particular church when there is one around the corner from where I live?' And if it should be a wealthy or famous person they might say, 'I want a personal audience with this person – I don't want to have to sit out in the audience like everybody else. Why should I take a chance risking my reputation?'

All these may seem reasonable questions. But it happens that the God of the Bible has chosen the foolish things of the world to confound the wise, the weak things of the world to shame the strong (1 Cor. 1:17–28). Like it or not, God said, 'For my thoughts are not your thoughts, neither are your ways my ways.' As a matter of fact, 'As the heavens are higher than the earth, so are my ways higher than your ways and my thoughts than your thoughts' (Isa. 55:8). I know people who say, 'If I become a Christian it won't be in *that* church or through *that* minister,' or, 'If I let anybody pray for me it will have to be so and so – nobody else.' I think God looks down and quietly passes over people who put those kind of demands on God.

I shudder to think where I would be today had I let my biases govern all my decisions over the years. I would have missed the most strategic moments of my life. Nearly fifty years ago I began to experience how God chooses servants who are utterly outside my 'camp' (see Heb. 13:13) to reach me. He has been doing it ever since. Nothing can be more deadly than provincialism – when we live in our own narrow community and fancy that 'if God is going to work it will happen with us'.

To their everlasting credit Naaman's own servants went to him, probably with fear and trembling, and said, 'If the prophet had told you to do some great thing, would you not have done it? How much more, then, when he tells you, "Wash and be cleansed"?' (2 Kings 5:13). In other words, they were gently showing Naaman that he had nothing to lose.

He climbed down. He went down to the river and 'dipped himself in the Jordan seven times, *as the man of God had told him*, and his flesh was restored and became clean like that of a young boy' (2 Kings 5:14). Then Naaman and all his attendants went back to the man of God – this time they got to meet Elisha personally – and said, 'Now I know that there is no God in all the world except in Israel' (2 Kings 5:15).

Naaman's tongue almost robbed him of one of the most extraordinary miracles in history.

5. *Nathanael, after being biased about the city where Jesus lived.*
Philip, having just been converted, went to Nathanael and said, 'We have found the one Moses wrote about in the Law, and about whom the prophets also wrote – Jesus of Nazareth, the son of Joseph.' Nathanael wasted no time retorting to this news, 'Nazareth! Can anything good come from there?' They replied, 'Come and see' (John 1:45–46).

Some people are prejudiced over a particular person, others object to a particular place. In England the typical southern Englishman seems to feel a cut above the northerner – from York or Manchester. But in America the northerner often looks down on people (like me) from Kentucky or Tennessee! We get used to an accent or style and become set in our ways. A person from New York or New England cannot imagine that a person with a 'hick' accent can have anything of substance to say!

But Philip insisted that Nathanael 'come and see' for himself. It was good advice. Once Nathanael became willing to meet Jesus, something unexpected occurred: Jesus saw him coming and said of him, 'Here is a true Israelite, in whom there is nothing false.' Astounded, Nathanael replied, 'How do you know me?' Jesus answered, 'I saw you while you were still under the fig-tree before Philip called you' (John 1:47–48).

Nothing is more calming to us than when we discover that God knows all about us. It gives us a good feeling of trust, that we are cared for. God knew exactly how to cut across Nathanael's prejudice.

In the early days when I was at Westminster Chapel a person came to hear me, dragging his feet, because his friends insisted on it. 'I will never be blessed by an American,' he said to them. It turned out that he had worked for some American bankers who had treated him unfairly. But he came. My sermon that day was on Jonah, when he was at sea in a storm and the sailors asked him, 'Who are you?' and Jonah replied, 'I am a Hebrew' (Jonah 1:8–9). Somehow my messaged tapped into that hostile man. He thought his friends had told me all about him. He sat on the pew afterwards crying. God broke down the barriers.

He has to do that with all of us. None of us would climb down from our fixed position were it not for the sheer grace of God.

So Nathanael climbed down. 'Rabbi, you are the Son of God; you are the King of Israel' (John 1:49). Had his friends not said, 'Come and see' and had Nathanael stuck to his guns, his life would never have been changed. His tongue almost kept him outside the kingdom.

6. *Thomas, who vowed not to believe that Jesus was raised from the dead unless he saw the nail prints in his hands.*
Thomas, one of the twelve disciples, was not present when Jesus showed himself alive to the disciples. I personally think he believed their report, 'We have seen the Lord!' (John 20:25). He knew they would not make up a story like that; they had been as discouraged over Jesus' crucifixion as he was.

I think he was just hurt. He felt cheated that he was not present when Jesus showed up. He was feeling sorry for himself and sulking, refusing to believe their account. 'Unless I see the nail marks in his hands and put my finger into his side, I will not believe it.' Strong words. I would not encourage anybody to talk like that! God owes us nothing, and the person who demands empirical proof of the Bible before he becomes a Christian will almost certainly never believe. You cannot bluff God.

But Jesus knew Thomas. He remembered he was but dust (Ps. 103:14). A week later Jesus did turn up and this time Thomas was present. Jesus singled out Thomas and graciously said to him, 'Put your finger here; see my hands. Reach out your hand and put it into my side. Stop doubting and believe' (John 20:27).

Thomas climbed down. He said to Jesus, 'My Lord and my God' (John 20:28). Thomas got it right with his tongue that time! But Jesus was the gracious one. Jesus by doing this let Thomas save face. God is like that. He could, if he chose, hold our words against us – and pass us by completely. But he is gracious and gives all of us a second chance.

7. *Ananias, as well as a number of other Christians, not believing Saul of Tarsus was converted.*

Saul's conversion took place with no Christians witnessing it. The last thing that Christians knew about Saul of Tarsus was that he was dedicated to exterminate every Christian alive! The first to receive the news of Saul's conversion did not hear it from a Christian but from the Lord himself.

In a vision Ananias was simply told, 'Go to the house of Judas on Straight Street and ask for a man from Tarsus named Saul, for he is praying.' Ananias wanted to argue – or, at least, he doubted whether he was having an authentic vision from the Holy Spirit. 'Lord, I have heard many reports about this man and all the harm he has done to your saints in Jerusalem. And he has come here with authority from the chief priests to arrest all who call on your name' (Acts 9:11–14). One sympathises with Ananias. It is consoling to me that you can question the Lord as Ananias did when it seemed so extraordinary.

But the Lord replied, 'Go! This man is my chosen instrument to carry my name before the Gentiles and their kings and before the people of Israel. I will show him how much he must suffer for my name' (Acts 9:15–16).

Ananias believed these words, climbed down, and went to Saul and prayed for him.

Christians everywhere were having the same problem. Rumours spread of Saul's conversion, but they thought it could be a set-up. When Saul came to Jerusalem, he tried to join the disciples, 'but they were all afraid of him, not believing that he really was a disciple' (Acts 9:26). This time it was Barnabas who made the apostles see that Saul was truly converted.

All eventually believed, climbed down, and the church everywhere 'enjoyed a time of peace' (Acts 9:31). The church was never the same again.

# 9

# In the Presence
# of an Enemy

You prepare a table before me in the presence of my
enemies.

*Ps. 23:5*

When Jesus said, 'Love your enemies' (Matt. 5:44) there was
an underlying assumption that we would have them! There
are, of course, degrees to which this is true. It could be a
longstanding enemy who wants to destroy you, a neighbour
who is always annoying, a rival who is jealous of you or
someone who is a temporary nuisance. But we all have
them, sooner or later. Tongue control with a person like this
is an extremely delicate test – and yet good practice for
other areas of our lives. Jesus said that the one who is faithful
in what is least will also be faithful in much (Luke 16:10).

I was preaching on total forgiveness in Northern Ireland

and a minister came up to me afterwards and said, 'Can your wife be your enemy?' I was slightly taken aback, having never been faced with that question before! But I answered: yes. When there are difficulties in marriage, the spouse often appears as an enemy. How one copes with words with one's husband or wife is crucial, but it is equally an opportunity for practising tongue control in all relationships.

## 1. *David, running from King Saul.*

The Bible says that David behaved himself wisely in all his ways (1 Sam. 18:14, KJV). This is stated right after his victory over Goliath, which gave him a new relationship with King Saul. Killing Goliath was both the best thing and the worst thing to happen to David at the time. It was good – it gave him favour with the king and the people. But his anointing was a severe threat to the king. The refrain, 'Saul has slain his thousands, and David his tens of thousands' (1 Sam. 18:7) made Saul go ballistic. He used up more energy in trying to hunt down and destroy David than he did fighting Israel's enemy – the Philistines. This is how perverse jealousy can cause one to be.

Behaving oneself wisely means taking the right decisions but mainly it refers to self-restraint with words. For the next twenty years David would learn self-control regarding the tongue. It was part of his preparation for the kingship. The great English preacher Charles Spurgeon once said, 'If I knew I had twenty-five years left to live I would spend twenty of it in preparation.' Dr Martyn Lloyd-Jones once said to me, 'The worst thing that can happen to a man is to succeed before he is ready.' King Saul succeeded before he was ready; he ended in utter failure. God was determined that David, a man after his own heart (1 Sam. 13:14), would not succeed until he was ready.

If you are wondering, 'Why do I have to wait so long before God will use me?' or perhaps you ask, 'Why is God taking so long to do what he promised?', the answer probably has to do with God overruling in your life in a manner that keeps you from being successful before you are ready. He is looking out for you; he knows your frame; he remembers that you are 'dust' (Ps. 103:14). So be encouraged. God is dealing with you in exactly the same manner in which he handled David. It is because he loves you too much to let you succeed before you are ready.

David began at once to practise restraint with the tongue. King Saul offered his daughter in marriage to David. David shrewdly responded as if he did not see through the king's motive, 'Who am I, and what is my family or my father's clan in Israel, that I should become the king's son-in-law?' (1 Sam. 18:18). That was the first hint that David was learning to survive away from home. It was the first proof that God's hand was on him. David knew that Saul hated him. From that moment on it was part of David's preparation for the kingship to develop skills he never knew he had: to survive when someone is out to get you.

Having an enemy is good for us. It keeps us on our toes. I can honestly say that my own anointing has been increased and refined by the presence of an enemy. I learned to see the enemy as God's way of preparing me. My first reaction was 'Why, Lord?' But I came to see why: it was for my good – to develop character, strength, perseverance and total forgiveness. I could never have written *Total Forgiveness* were it not for the fact that I had to forgive utterly and totally those who wanted to hurt me.

On two occasions David had opportunity to get personal vengeance on the king – and he turned down the chance both times. 'I will not lift my hand against my master, because he is the Lord's anointed,' he said to King Saul (1 Sam. 24:10). David was steadfast in not giving the slightest occasion for the king to fault him. On the second occasion David refused to let his men destroy Saul because David knew that Saul's future, and his own future, was in God's hands. 'The Lord himself will strike him; either his time will come and he will die, or he will go into battle and perish. But the Lord forbid that I should lay a hand on the Lord's anointed. Now get the spear and water jug that are near his head, and let's go' (1 Sam. 26:10–11).

Turning down the second opportunity to destroy Saul was also a testimony to his loyal followers. These men could never forget this. It showed David's true character. When we have enemies, we also usually have some followers. How we behave toward our enemies in the presence of our followers is important. It is a testimony to what we are really like. David would pen those words from what is perhaps his most beloved psalm, 'You prepare a table before me in the presence of my enemies' (Ps. 23:5). How we behave toward our enemy will be noted by all who look on. It is a part of God refining us because he isn't finished with us yet.

2. *The Israelites, refusing to speak under the evil threat of Sennacherib.*

The king of Assyria sent his forces into Jerusalem to address Hezekiah the king and the common people who sat on the wall. These soldiers shouted insults to Israel's God and to the king. They hoped to cause a revolt among the ordinary people. 'Now do not let Hezekiah deceive you and mislead you like this. Do not believe him, for no god of any nation or kingdom has been able to deliver his people from my hand or the hand of my fathers. How much less will your god deliver you from my hand!' (2 Chron. 32:15).

Hezekiah sent word to Sennacherib's men not to speak in Hebrew to the people. Hezekiah was fearful that the people would weaken and give in. It was the greatest national crisis during the reign of King Hezekiah.

But King Hezekiah need not have worried. It was a grand and historic moment. 'But the people remained silent and *said nothing* in reply, because the king had commanded, "Do not answer him"' (Isa. 36:21). It was a wonderful moment. It was a beautiful sign of unity in Israel that not one person succumbed to Sennacherib's men. Shortly afterwards God supernaturally defeated Israel's enemies and Sennacherib's own people cut him down (Isa. 36:36–38).

Satan will always try to persuade the people of God to interact with him and negotiate with him. The Bible says, 'Resist the devil, and he will flee from you' (Js 4:7). When you feel pressured to speak, remember this account in Scripture. In such cases, when the exact word is not given to you, the best thing to do is to *say nothing*.

3. *Moses, having to face double opposition – from his own people and from Pharaoh.*

There is a sense in which every church leader is in continual threat of two-fold opposition – from within and without. The greater enemy of course is the world out there that needs to be confronted and converted. We must never forget the greater enemy and never fall into the trap King Saul fell into – of becoming more concerned about his personal enemy David than he was about the Philistines.

The devil would prefer that we are more concerned about opposition to our personal leadership than we are about marching into Satan's territory to bear witness to our Lord Jesus Christ.

But every Christian leader knows what it is to have opposition from within the circle of those they are leading. There will be those, almost always, who question your leadership – your wisdom, your decisions; and sometimes there is a bit of jealousy behind the whole thing that you have to contend with.

We saw earlier that Moses lost control of his temper on an important occasion towards the sunset years of his life, and ended up having to forgo entering the Promised Land. But he still had some forty years of impeccable leadership, showing all of us who are leaders the best way to handle those we lead. He was a pioneer leader, but eventually became almost too exalted among the Israelites. I sometimes wonder if God permitted Moses to make a big mistake at last to keep everybody from idolising him. Sometimes I think God sometimes lets a leader fail, lest people admire them too much!

Moses experienced every conceivable kind of opposition. He knew what it was for his following to turn from hot to cold in their attitude and loyalty to him. When he first appeared to the children of Israel as their appointed and anointed leader, he announced what God had revealed to him, then performed signs before them. The people believed. And when they heard that the Lord was concerned about them and had seen their misery, they bowed down and worshipped. It was a good beginning.

But after Moses' first confrontation with Pharaoh, which Moses hoped would mean an immediate emancipation for all the people to leave Egypt, what he got instead was a command for the people to find their own straw for making bricks – and keep up the same quota. The people of Israel turned not against Pharaoh but against Moses. 'May the Lord look upon you and judge you! You have made us a stench to Pharaoh and his officials and have put a sword in their hand to kill us' (Exod. 5:21).

Moses' reaction was that he said nothing back to them but turned to the Lord. God has big shoulders. I have often marvelled at David's words, 'I pour out my complaint' to the Lord (Ps. 142:2). This is what leaders must do. Instead of snapping back, or complaining to their people, they must pour out their complaints to God. God can cope with the pressure.

One of the greatest tests for Moses was having both his own people and the armies of Pharaoh coming against him simultaneously. How many of us who are leaders could cope well with that? Having been granted permission to leave Egypt, following the first Passover, the children of Israel had come to the edge of the Red Sea. Having assumed that they were finally rid of the bondage of Pharaoh, here came his armies marching towards Moses as the children of Israel were trapped with nowhere to go. If that wasn't enough, his own people turned against Moses and said, 'Was it because there were no graves in Egypt that you brought us to the desert to die? . . . It would have been better for us to serve the Egyptians than to die in the desert!' (Exod. 14:11–12).

Moses might have retorted, giving these ungrateful and unworthy people a piece of his mind. He controlled his tongue. He had presence of mind and answered the people, 'Do not be afraid, stand firm and you will see the deliverance the Lord will bring you today. The Egyptians you see today you will never see again. The Lord will fight for you; you need only to be still' (Exod. 14:13–14).

The truth is, despite this brave face, Moses was scared. I say this because in the very next verse the Lord said to Moses, 'Why are you crying out to me?' (Exod. 14:15). This can only mean that Moses had just cried to the Lord, even if it was only in his heart. It is as though there might have been a verse that said, 'Moses cried to the Lord' right after he said those gracious words to the children of Israel.

God stepped in, and told Moses: 'Raise your staff and stretch out your hand over the sea to divide the water so that the Israelites can go through the sea on dry ground.' They did. And the rest, as they say, is history.

4. *The counsel of Jesus when called to testify before governors and kings.*
Jesus said:

> Be on your guard against men; they will hand you over to the local councils and flog you in their synagogues. On my account you will be brought before governors and kings as witnesses to them and to the Gentiles. But when they arrest you, do not worry about what to say or how to say it. At that time you will be given what to say, for it will not be you speaking, but the Spirit of your Father speaking through you.
>
> Matt. 10:17–20

I will never forget the first time I took serious notice of this passage. I was pastor of a small church in Ohio where my teaching was brought under question. They claimed not to have a creed or statement of faith: 'only the Bible', they said to me. But when I preached from the Bible they rejected me, at least a large number of them. I was called in on the carpet by the ministers in the area.

On the day I was to face their charges I opened my Bible and unexpectedly these words from Matthew 10:17–20 leaped out at me. I knew then that God would be with me and that what I was having to do was similar to what Jesus said would happen. I was amazed at myself that night; I hardly spoke! But what I said nobody refuted. The ministers urged the people to try being nice and to get on with one another. I left a few months after that, but I can never forget how God saw me through that evening.

I quoted these words to Yasser Arafat when I saw him just a month or so before he died. I told him that I claimed those words every time I visited him (five times) and that what I said to him was not me but Jesus! He smiled and seemed to accept what I said. He knew too that I never entered the political arena, I stayed entirely with the gospel of Jesus and his death on the cross for our sins.

The point is this. When we need words in an emergency or special occasion, God is capable of giving us the exact words we need. If one does not carry an agenda on such an occasion, not thinking in advance what to say but letting the Spirit take control, it is amazing what comes out of our mouths!

In other words, Matthew 10:20 – 'it will not be you speaking' – is the only time I know of where we are *guaranteed* grace to control the tongue to that degree. I wish I could claim that verse twenty-four hours a day, seven days a week, but, alas, Matthew 10:20 is only promised for 'emergency grace'. In any case, Matthew 10:20 shows that

God certainly knows the right word! Indeed, 'from the Lord comes the reply of the tongue' (Prov. 16:1).

4. *Stephen, speaking before the Sanhedrin.*
Matthew 10:20 is exactly what was in full operation on the occasion when Stephen spoke, having been maligned and falsely accused (see Acts 6:11–14). Most of Acts 7 is Luke's report of Stephen's defence. It is a brilliant survey of Old Testament history with particular reference to a long tradition of opposition to the latest move of God.

And yet Stephen could not have spoken like that had he not also known his Old Testament. What was happening was the Holy Spirit bringing to his remembrance what he had learned (John 14:26). Let no one think that he or she can stand up and speak like this if the knowledge is not first imbedded in the heart and mind! We may think that if we are Spirit-filled then God will pour knowledge into our heads. If only! I would have to say kindly that if we are empty-headed before we are Spirit-filled we will be empty-headed afterwards. There *is* a place for Scripture memorisation, reading good books and sitting under sound teaching. When the Holy Spirit comes down on a people in power it will be on those who took the trouble to *learn* when it may not have seemed inspirational or easy.

5. *Jesus, when forced to testify before the chief priest, Herod and Pilate.*
I have long been fascinated by Paul's words, that our Lord Jesus, testifying before Pontius Pilate 'made the good confession' (1 Tim. 6:13).

Jesus never said anything wrong the whole of his life. He was sinless – in thought, word and deed. So it is in a sense redundant to say that he spoke the words from the Father when standing before Herod and Pilate. All he ever did was this. 'The Son can do nothing by himself; he can do only what he sees his Father doing, because whatever the Father does the Son also does' (John 5:19). Therefore the Spirit of the Father was always the explanation for his perfect words.

And yet Jesus gives us the perfect example of tongue control in the presence of the enemy before Herod, the high priest and Pilate. There are two things that contributed to this 'good confession': the timing of his silence and the choice of his words. 'As a sheep before her shearers is silent, so he did not open his mouth' (Isa. 53:7). When he was brought in to Herod, the latter 'plied him with many questions, but Jesus gave him no answer' (Luke 23:9). It demonstrates that he had no fear whatever.

It takes a lot of confidence and courage to say *absolutely nothing*. That utter silence was partly what made Jesus' testimony before the authorities so stunning. It demonstrated his total peace, confidence and self-control.

But Jesus ended up answering the high priest because he faced a different situation with him. The high priest stood up and said to Jesus, 'Are you not going to answer? What is this testimony that these men are bringing against you?' But Jesus remained silent. However, Jesus was required to speak when the high priest said to him, 'I charge you under oath by the living God: tell us if you are the Christ, the Son of God.' Jesus replied: 'Yes, it is as you say' (Matt. 26:62–64).

Why did Jesus speak to the high priest? He had to. He had put himself under the Law (Matt. 5:17; Gal. 4:4) and therefore had no choice. The Law said, 'If a person sins because he does not speak up when he hears a public charge to testify regarding something he has seen or learned about,

he will be held responsible' (Lev. 5:1). This is why he spoke
to the high priest. I had not made the connection between
Matthew 26:64 and Leviticus 5:1 until Richard Roe, a
deacon at Westminster Chapel, shared this with me.

Regarding Pilate, Jesus maintained silence with him for a
while. When asked, 'Where do you come from,' Jesus gave
no answer. But when Pilate said, 'Don't you realise I have
power either to free you or to crucify you?' Jesus chose to
answer, 'You would have no power over me if it were not
given to you from above. Therefore the one who handed me
over to you is guilty of a greater sin' (John 19:9–11).

In answering these words to Pilate Jesus affirmed the
state. It is the New Testament position that the authorities
that exist are ordained of God (Rom. 13:1). Jesus was an
example of how we are to respect law and government, even
if we do not always agree with who is in power. Paul called
his witness a good confession.

# 10

# Dignifying the Trial

> Consider it pure joy, my brothers, whenever you face trials
> of many kinds.
>
> *Js 1:2*

In the autumn of 1979, less than three years after starting my ministry at Westminster Chapel, I began a series of sermons on the book of James. I planned this series for several weeks. We had a six-week vacation, part of which was at Disneyworld. We had been the year before as it happens, and I wasn't particularly looking forward to going back. But our children were eager to do so, so of course we went. To be there was one minor consolation. I recalled the best pizza I ever ate when we were there the previous year, at a pizza parlour in Kissimmee, Florida. I will get that again, I promised everybody.

After we checked into our motel, we travelled to the pizza place, about six blocks away. Louise, T. R., Melissa and

I put in our orders. I ordered the 'deluxe' with everything imaginable on it, including anchovies. After a good while the pizza was still not ready. I went to the counter and asked about it. They did not have my order. A new man came on a shift. 'So what do you want?' they said – not bothering to apologise. I did not exactly radiate the love of Jesus, but grudgingly called the family up and we ordered again. It finally came, and when I paid I did not smile, neither was tongue control in operation. We had been there about forty-five minutes.

When we came outside it was pouring with rain – a real tropical downpour. But we dashed to the car, getting wet. But we all thought it was worth it – those pizzas were going to be so good! Louise, T. R. and Melissa took their pizzas and ran to the room (we were parked in front of it). When I got out, I stepped into a foot of water. I opened the back door and water poured on my pizza – and the sack that was carrying it was drenched and the whole pizza fell out into the water – the whole thing: sausage, pepperoni, peppers, cheese, mushrooms, onions and anchovies!

My verbal response to this was not my finest hour.

If I was to eat anything, I had no choice but to go back – and re-order. I immediately thought of having to face the man to whom I was not the epitome of Christ-likeness.

But an amazing thing happened during the six-block drive to the pizza restaurant. My mind immediately went to James 1:2, 'Count it all joy when ye fall into diverse temptations' (KJV). I said to myself, 'Either what I preach is true or it isn't,' and I wanted my earliest sermons on James to launch the series in good fashion. The phrase *dignify the trial* came into my head. I immediately determined to dignify that trial. It seems so silly now, but it was literally a life-changing moment for me and the beginning of an era that continues to the present day, in which I have sought as faithfully as possible to dignify every trial God allowed me to have. I apologised to the man at the pizza place. I was so ashamed. He made another – and didn't even charge me!

I began to think about how many years had gone by (I was 44 then) in which I had done nothing but murmur, complain and grumble through every trial that ever came my way – however great or small. I felt so ashamed. But I vowed that day – and I have sought hard every day since, not always succeeding, to keep that vow. As I write these lines I am seventy. I still make every effort to focus on dignifying any trial God allows to come my way. Laugh if you will, but it all began with the pizza incident!

People hear our words. My family hears my words. The angels hear our words. God hears our words.

Dignifying the trial means accepting any trial graciously as being a gift of God, going through it all without complaining, and letting it last as long as necessary to accomplish God's purpose in it. All trials do end. When the trial is over we either pass or fail in the sight of God. When God says 'well done' at the end of the trial it means not only that sweet affirmation but an increased anointing. What determines our grade? Our words.

1. *Abraham, when told to sacrifice his son Isaac to the Lord.*
Abraham is called the father of the faithful (Rom. 4:11). He was Paul's chief example for justification by faith but also for receiving an inheritance. Both teachings are in Romans 4. I happen to believe that the key to the next great move of God on the earth is the book of Romans, especially

chapter 4. Abraham was justified by his faith in the promise (Gen. 15:6), but he received an inheritance by accepting that his true heir would come from Sarah's womb (Rom. 4:18–21).

But there was more testing for Abraham. Few people have suffered like Abraham. But suffering is not for nothing. The greater the suffering, the greater the anointing. One day God told Abraham to sacrifice his son Isaac (Gen. 22:1–2). I cannot imagine a trial greater than that. Abraham not only obeyed, but dignified this unthinkable trial by his words. Sometimes God asks us to do things that make no sense at all at the time. Abraham had witnesses – two of his servants – before whom Abraham would also bear witness. But he did not say to anybody what was happening, where they were going or why; he was quietly obeying the Lord.

When asked by his little boy Isaac, knowing there would be a sacrifice of some sort – because they were taking wood for the burnt offering, 'Where is the lamb for the burnt offering?' Abraham answered, 'God himself will provide the lamb for the burnt offering, my son' (Gen. 22:8). This must have been the hardest moment of all for Abraham. He could have lost control of his emotions and words here. But there was no talk of, 'How could God do this to me?' 'This is not fair' or 'This doesn't make sense.' There was no sulking. He simply obeyed. That is dignifying the trial.

Abraham fully intended to carry through with God's order. But he was stopped by the Lord himself at the last moment, 'Do not lay a hand on the boy . . . Now I know that you fear God, because you have not withheld from me your son, your only son' (Gen. 22:12).

The consequence of this was one of the greatest spiritual

experiences that ever can be given to a human being on this planet – namely, to have God swear an oath to you. 'I swear by myself . . . I will surely bless you and make your descendants as numerous as the stars in the sky and as the sand on the seashore' (Gen. 22:16–17).

When we bless the Lord by tongue control, he blesses us by telling us what we want to know – and a thousand times more than we could dream of. Dignifying the trial is a promised route to those who desire a greater walk with God and a greater anointing of the Holy Spirit on their lives.

2. *Leah, who learned to dignify her trial with words.*
Leah was Jacob's unwanted wife – he had been tricked into taking her (see Gen. 29:16–30) – and the woman he never loved or appreciated. She was a rival to her beautiful sister Rachel – who was very much loved by Jacob. There was one compensation for Leah: she could bear children when Rachel could not.

But one of the strong motives she had for wanting children was the hope that, at long last, Jacob would love and appreciate her. When she gave birth to Reuben, she said, 'It is because the Lord has seen my misery. Surely my husband will love me now' (Gen. 29:32). But he apparently didn't.

She gave birth to another son – Simeon, and said, 'Because the Lord heard that I am not loved, he gave me this one too' (Gen. 29:33).

Her fourth child was Levi. When he was born she said, 'Now at last my husband will become attached to me, because I have borne him three sons' (Gen. 29:34). But there was no reason why having these three sons made any difference to Jacob. He loved Rachel.

God wanted to teach Leah that *he* loved her, even if Jacob did not. The entire ordeal was part of God's preparation for Leah – but also the church – that he is behind all that happens to us.

She had one more son – Judah. I find her words so moving, I can hardly read them without coming to tears: 'This time I will praise the Lord' (Gen. 29:35). Those words went up to Heaven like sweet incense. She dignified her trial with words that reveal she had come to terms with what was not going to happen – winning her husband's love – and what had already happened – having the Lord love her so much.

Which of the sons do you suppose became the greatest blessing to Israel down the road? Whereas Rachel eventually gave birth to Joseph and Benjamin, the two sons that gave the church the ultimate gift were Levi – from which sprang the Levitical priesthood – and Judah, the tribe that produced Israel's Messiah and our Lord and Saviour Jesus Christ.

Leah's blessing, though it was not what she wanted, turned out to be the greater blessing to the church. When she said, 'This time I will praise the Lord,' she could not have known that God had strategically placed her in a position to bless his people through her more than ever. And she remains an example to all of us, especially unloved women, who can learn to dignify the trial through words.

3. *Eli, upon hearing most disquieting words about his legacy.*
Eli was the high priest at the time Samuel was born. When Samuel was a little boy, he heard from God one night – but did not know what to make of it at first. When God called Samuel, he answered, 'Here I am,' but ran to Eli, not thinking God would speak to Samuel directly. But Eli

replied that he had not spoken and told the young Samuel to go back to bed.

But it happened again; the Lord called, 'Samuel!' and he got up and went to Eli and said, 'Here I am; you called me.' But Eli said again, 'I did not call; go back and lie down.' But when it happened a third time, Eli – to his everlasting credit – recognised the movement of the Holy Spirit, and ordered Samuel, 'God and lie down, and if he calls you, say, "Speak, Lord, for your servant is listening."' And Samuel went back to bed (1 Sam. 3:1–9).

Eli is one of the unsung heroes in the Old Testament. I used to talk about him with Dr Martyn Lloyd-Jones, one of my predecessors at Westminster Chapel. 'I always liked him and felt for him,' Dr Lloyd-Jones used to say to me. Eli had brought up two sons, destined from birth to be priests, but both of them went badly wrong. They were a grief to the ageing Eli (1 Sam. 2:22–25).

When Samuel returned to bed that night,

The Lord came and stood there, calling as at the other times, 'Samuel! Samuel!' Then Samuel said, 'Speak, for your servant is listening' And the Lord said to Samuel: 'See, I am about to do something in Israel that will make the ears of everyone who hears of it tingle . . . I will carry out against Eli everything I spoke against his family – from beginning to end. For I told him that I would judge his family for ever because of the sin he knew about; his sons made themselves contemptible, and he failed to restrain them. Therefore I swore to the house of Eli, "The guilt of Eli's house will never be atoned for by sacrifice or offering."'

1 Sam. 3:10–14

Those were awful words to have to hear. But Eli heard them because he demanded that little Samuel tell him every word, which he did – hiding nothing from him. And yet it became a brilliant moment for Eli. It showed there was something good left in the old man after all, for he dignified this enormous trial with these words: 'He is the Lord; let him do what is good in his eyes' (1 Sam. 3:18). His sons died shortly afterwards in the battle. The Philistines captured the ark of God, and when Eli heard that the ark was taken he fell and died at the age of ninety-eight (1 Sam. 4:18).

The best way we can dignify a trial – however heavy it may be – is by words that affirm the wisdom and judgement of God. God likes it when we bless him in this manner. First, that we recognise God at work – 'it is the Lord' – and, secondly, that we bend the knee: 'let him do what is good in his eyes.' If all else that has proceeded is bad, and very bad, speaking like that is not a bad way to end.

4. *King David, during his exile.*
One of the most sublime examples of dignifying a trial with words was when King David, leaving Jerusalem in humiliation, was cursed by a man called Shimei. He pelted David with stones, despite David being guarded. As he cursed, Shimei shouted, 'Get out, get out, you man of blood, you scoundrel! The Lord has repaid you for all the blood you shed in the household of Saul, in whose place you have reigned. The Lord has handed the kingdom over to your son Absalom. You have come to ruin because you are a man of blood' (2 Sam. 16:7–8).

This would be pretty tough to have to listen to. It was

probably the worst thing David could hear at a time like
this, if only because he would be the first to admit there was
some truth in these words.

I know what it is to receive criticism, sometimes very
unjust. But fifty years of ministry have taught me to listen to
my critics. Even though their motives may not be the best,
sometimes you learn from them and have to admit that
some of their words have truth in them.

How did David dignify this trial with words? David said
to his officials (who could have got immediate vengeance),
'My son, who is of my own flesh, is trying to take my life.
How much more, then, this Benjamite! Leave him alone; let
him curse, for the Lord has told him to. It may be that the
Lord will see my distress and repay me with good for the
cursing I am receiving today' (2 Sam. 16:11–12). Shimei
continued on and on with his cursing. David controlled his
tongue.

5. *Jehoshaphat, praising God in the midst of the battle.*
This king of Judah was given some disquieting news: 'A vast
army is coming against you from Edom' (2 Chron. 20:2).
Alarmed, Jehoshaphat resolved to seek the Lord and
proclaimed a fast for all Judah. The people all responded.
Jehoshaphat was given a prophetic word: 'You will not have
to fight this battle . . . Do not be afraid; do not be discouraged. Go out to face them tomorrow, and the Lord will be
with you' (2 Chron. 20:17).

What was Jehoshaphat's response? He took the prophetic
word seriously and went to his people: 'Listen to me, Judah
and people of Jerusalem! Have faith in the Lord your God
and you will be upheld; have faith in his prophets and you
will be successful' (2 Chron. 20:20). At that point the king

did something most extraordinary; he appointed men to *sing* to the Lord and to praise him

> for the splendour of his holiness as they went out at the head of the army, saying: 'Give thanks to the Lord, for his love endures for ever.'
>
> 2 Chron. 20:21

This is one of those video replays I look forward to seeing when I get to Heaven. *As they began to sing and praise*, the Lord stepped in with a particular strategy by which Judah defeated the enemy. The lesson for us: God loves praise. Thank him in the darkest hour. Trust the word he has given. This way he does the fighting for us.

### 6. *The apostles, after they left the Sanhedrin.*

Peter and the apostles had been put in jail for preaching the gospel, but they were miraculously set free and commenced preaching again in the temple courts (Acts 5:17–20). They were arrested again and warned about teaching in the name of Jesus. Peter and the apostles replied, 'We must obey God rather than men!' (Acts 5:29).

A Pharisee named Gamaliel stood up in the Sanhedrin and cautioned the Jews not to be too hard on them – lest they be fighting against God. His speech persuaded them, but they still had the apostles flogged, and commanded not to speak in the name of Jesus, before they were let go (Acts 5:33–40).

Here are some of the most moving words in the book of Acts: the apostles left the Sanhedrin, 'rejoicing because they had been counted worthy of suffering disgrace for the Name' (Acts 5:41). I love the way the KJV put it: they rejoiced that they were counted worthy 'to suffer shame for his name'.

The Jews probably thought they had taught Peter and his friends a lesson, that the strong words and flogging would succeed in keeping them quiet – and make them feel ashamed.

They could not have known that the opposite was true. The apostles couldn't believe their luck, if I may put it that way. They regarded suffering for the shame of the name of Jesus as a very high honour – they did not feel worthy of this! But they were getting it! You might question, therefore, whether this is dignifying the trial. It was something they welcomed. That makes it no trial. But of course it was a trial. It hurt. But the privilege of rejoicing in it transcended the pain and disgrace so that they were honoured to have this.

A ninety-year-old lady once said to a friend of mine years ago, 'I have been serving the Lord so long that I can hardly tell the difference between a blessing and a trial.'

When you dignify a trial with rejoicing it is not only a blessing; it leads to greater honour and blessing. The early church was just beginning at that time. Far, far more was to come. So too with us. Welcoming a trial, rather than rejecting it, augurs well for our future. We prove that we accept it graciously by what we say.

7. *Jesus, accepting God's will in Gethsemane.*
The writer of Hebrews was partly referring to Jesus in Gethsemane when he said, 'He offered up prayers and petitions with loud cries and tears' and also that he 'learned obedience from what he suffered' (Heb. 5:7–9). The latter

phrase is something I do not profess to understand, I just believe it.

At any rate, Jesus was the supreme example of dignifying a trial. While in Gethsemane, anticipating the cross, his agony was so great that 'his sweat was like drops of blood falling to the ground' (Luke 22:44). But it was in Gethsemane that he settled it finally that there was no other way to proceed but by the cross. He prayed, 'My Father, if it is possible, may this cup be taken from me. Yet not as I will, but as you will' (Matt. 26:39).

Dignifying the trial is accepting the wisdom, verdict and will of God without complaining. The prayer of Jesus in Gethsemane lets us know that we don't wish for a trial. In the Lord's Prayer we are told to pray, 'Lead us not into temptation' (Matt. 6:13). The Greek word *peirasmos* is translated either temptation or trial. We should always pray not to enter into temptation or trial, but we must dignify such if it must come.

However, Jesus apparently hoped to have a little company with him during this ordeal. He took Peter, James and John with him. I take the view that he was lonely, feeling the anguish and somehow hoped that the pain might be slightly lessened to have these three men with him as on previous occasions.

But they slept through it all. He gently rebuked them, 'Could you men not keep watch with me for one hour?' (Matt. 26:40). But they went back to sleep. When he went through this the third time he came to terms with the fact that he would experience both Gethsemane and the crucifixion utterly alone. I am touched by the way the KJV puts it in Matthew 26:45: 'Sleep on now, and take your rest.' However much he wanted to have them alongside, he knew he had to give this wish up.

He did not let them lose face. He simply said, 'The Son of Man is betrayed into the hands of sinners. Rise, let us go!' (Matt. 26:45–46). There was no self-pity, no grumbling, only dignity. He was not only our sinless substitute in his death, but also our perfect example of how we are to live our lives and control the tongue.

# 11

# Total Forgiveness

Another reason for forgiveness is to keep from being outsmarted by Satan; for we know what he is trying to do.

*2 Cor. 2:11, LB*

The best preparation and training for tongue control is practising total forgiveness. Total forgiveness is the quickest way to ensure that the Holy Spirit is not grieved (Eph. 4:30–32), and when the *ungrieved* Spirit of God indwells us in greater and greater measure, the art of tongue control is more likely to be developed in us.

1. *Joseph, when he revealed his identity to his brothers who had betrayed him.*
Because of dreams the Lord gave him (Gen. 37:5–11), Joseph always knew that one day his brothers would bow down to him. Because of their jealousy and hatred toward him they sold him to the Ishmaelites, never expecting to see

him again. But twenty-two years later Joseph's dreams were perfectly fulfilled. He had even become Prime Minister of Egypt and these brothers had to come to Egypt to buy food. Joseph immediately recognised them but they did not recognise him. He spoke through an interpreter. But the moment came when he could bear it no longer and decided to reveal his identity to them.

He always assumed he could look at those brothers, say 'Gotcha!' and then throw the book at them and see them punished. But a new Joseph had emerged. He had totally forgiven them. How do we know?

First, he ensured that nobody would ever know what they did to him. He made everybody but the eleven brothers leave the room (Gen. 45:1). Behind closed doors he revealed who he was. He made sure nobody – ever – would find out what the brothers had done. Total forgiveness is *not telling anybody* what people have done to you. The way we normally 'punish' those who hurt us is to make sure people know what 'they' did to us. We try to get even by destroying their credibility – telling as many as we can find what they did. We cannot bear that people would admire those who have hurt us.

Joseph would not let them be afraid of him. 'Come close to me,' he urged them, knowing they were terrified of him (Gen. 45:3–4). He would not even let them feel guilty. 'Do not be distressed and do not be angry with yourselves for selling me here' (Gen. 45:5). Most of us want to make sure that people feel guilty – and feel very sorry – before we forgive them.

He let them save face. 'It was not you who sent me here, but God' (Gen. 45:8). He protected their egos, their self-esteem – even covering up for them to make them feel better. Joseph even protected them from their dark secret, namely, them letting their father Jacob think a wild animal had killed Joseph. He would not let them tell their father what really happened (Gen. 45:9–11).

Finally, Joseph's forgiveness was something that lasted. Seventeen years later Jacob died. The brothers panicked and feared that Joseph would at last get vengeance on them. Never! He demonstrated that he still forgave them (Gen. 50:15–21). Total forgiveness is a 'life sentence'; we do it as long as we live.

How did the brothers know Joseph forgave them? He *said* things that indicated there was no grudge, no bitterness. His *words* made them *feel* forgiven. They were thrilled. You only verbalise forgiveness, however, when the people need and want it. If they don't want it you still must forgive them. But don't tell them in this case. Never say 'I forgive you' unless you know for sure it is what they yearn to hear from you. Otherwise they will resent it and accuse you of pointing the finger. Total forgiveness is articulated in such a manner that shows there is no bitterness in you whatever. For more details see *Total Forgiveness*.

2. *Moses, interceding before God on behalf of a people who rejected his leadership.*
I have said that Moses was the greatest leader of people in human history. And this is partly why. It was not merely his ability. He was a man who practised total forgiveness. The Spirit of God was in him *ungrieved*. This is why he had constant two-way communication with God.

An opportunity was handed to Moses by God on a silver platter that most leaders I know would have taken with both hands. God said to Moses in so many words, 'Moses, this is a sorry lot you have for a following. They are not accepting your leadership or mine. I have decided to wipe them all out entirely and start all over again with you and together we will build a new nation' (see Num. 14:11–12).

I would hate to think what I might have done had God said that to me in any of the churches of which I have been the minister. This includes all six churches I have led, including Westminster Chapel. I have had opposition to some degree in every single one of these churches. When it became very difficult, had God said to me what he said to Moses, I would not want you to know what comes to my mind! I may well have taken God up on his offer.

But not Moses. NO! he thundered back:

> Then the Egyptians will hear about it! By your power you brought these people up from among them. And they will tell the inhabitants of this land about it. They have already heard that you, O Lord, are with these people . . . If you put these people to death all at one time, the nations who have heard this report about you will say, 'The Lord was not able to bring these people into the land he promised them on oath . . . In accordance with your great love, forgive the sin of these people . . .'
>
> Num. 14:13–19

I call that greatness. I would have to say that this moment was probably the greatest example of true greatness recorded by God or man in all human history. Greatness is not success or fame. Greatness is accepting the worst possible conditions and dignifying God through it all. I think of the words of Psalm 106:23: 'So he said he would destroy them – had not Moses . . . *stood in the breach* before him to keep his wrath from destroying them.'

This is why God trusted Moses with so much authority, power, favour and fame. To the degree we forgive totally God will entrust us with a greater anointing. By the way, what do you suppose happened then? God forgave them!

Moses was not concerned about his personal ego or how he would look. He was concerned about the honour of God's name – and how the peoples of the earth would look at God.

3. *Stephen, interceding for his killers just before he died.*

We had a brief look above at Stephen's speech before the Sanhedrin. I did not mention how Stephen's face was aglow 'like the face of an angel' (Acts 6:15). We pointed out Stephen's grasp of Israelite history and how he used the moment to warn us that there is not only continuity with the blessing of God in history; there is sadly also continuity with opposition to what God is in. There are two kinds of heritages, you might say.

When I had opposed the 'Toronto Blessing' and listened to Ken Costa, churchwarden of Holy Trinity, Brompton tell me what was happening in his church, I suddenly had a strange feeling that I myself was about to fill out one more chapter in opposing the latest movement of the Spirit. O Lord, I thought, please don't let me do this. As soon as I saw that, I climbed down. The thesis of Stephen's reply to the Sanhedrin was precisely this.

I have marvelled at Stephen's anointing; one of the original seven deacons – an example for every layman and every church leader in Scripture. What was the explanation for such ostensible radiance, power and wisdom? I think I know. It is seen in Stephen's final seconds. As he was being stoned – a horrible way to die – Stephen's very last words were these: 'Lord do not hold this sin against them' (Acts 7:60).

Many of us, knowing that we are to pray for our enemies, will pray something like, 'Lord I commit them to you.' I think God must be annoyed at such a prayer. The way he wants us to pray for those who have hurt us, however unjust they were, is that they would be let *off the hook*. That they will be blessed rather than cursed. That is what God asks us to do.

When we do that, we demonstrate total forgiveness.

Stephen was also emulating our Lord Jesus Christ in his final moments. We therefore look at one more example of this kind of graciousness.

4. *Jesus, praying for those who crucified him.*
The most frequent criticism I receive about my book *Total Forgiveness* is my point that you must not wait until others repent or are sorry before you forgive them. These people want to say that we surely are not required to forgive people who have not repented first! I reply: nine out of ten people you ever have to forgive don't even think they have done anything wrong! So what are you to do, go to them and point out how wrong they are? Hardly.

All four of these examples show, one at a time, that we are not allowed the luxury of waiting until they repent first. First, Joseph told the brothers, 'Do not be angry with yourselves.' Second, the children of Israel were not the slightest bit bothered over their rebellion when Moses prayed for them. Third, how sorry do you suppose these Jews were who were stoning Stephen?

So when Jesus prayed for those who crucified him, how

much repentance do you find at his cross? They laughed, they scoffed, 'Come down from the cross, that we may see and believe' (Mark 15:32). 'He saved others . . . but he cannot save himself' (Matt. 27:42). In fact, not only did they not repent; they were so sure they were right in doing this that they said, 'His blood be on us and our children!' (Matt. 27:25).

Jesus' response to all of this was: 'Father, forgive them, for they do not know what they are doing' (Luke 23:34). I agree with Dr G. Campbell Morgan, one of my predecessors at Westminster Chapel, who said he expects to see in Heaven the very people who drove in the nails. I would go further. I think that when we get to Heaven we will find that those who were converted at Pentecost included many of these people who were active in Jesus' demise.

It takes minimal grace to forgive when people are sorry. 'A gentle answer [soft words, KJV] turns away wrath' (Prov. 15:1). Even cold-hearted and wicked people can find it easy to forgive when the person is truly sorry. So forgiving people when they are sorry is no evidence whatever of the Spirit of God in you. But when you forgive them when they are *not* sorry – or when they don't even think they have done anything wrong, that shows grace indeed. That is what Moses, Stephen and Jesus did. It is what we are required to do. And don't be surprised that God answers our prayer and forgives them – and lets them off the hook! 'Oh no,' you may say. Oh yes! That is the point!

We have a gracious God. 'Be merciful, just as your father is merciful' (Luke 6:36). This is true godliness. Not how plainly you dress, what cinemas you don't attend, what things you give up or how often you go to church; it is total forgiveness and being merciful just as God is.

It is our *words* that indicate whether we are bitter or loving. This is why Jesus said, 'For by your words you will be acquitted, and by your words you will be condemned' (Matt. 12:37). You may have evil thoughts. Yes, we all have them. But we don't have to say them. 'You might as well say what you think,' some keep saying. Wrong. It is our tongues that get us into trouble. Controlling the tongue is the goal.

And likewise it is the *tongue* by which we bless people and honour the Lord.

# Part Three
# The Trouble with
# the Tongue

We all stumble in many ways. If anyone is never at fault in
what he says, he is a perfect man, able to keep his whole
body in check.

*Js 3:2*

Every mistake I have ever made, every sin I have ever
committed and every sense of guilt that continues to give
me grief and pain can be traced to my own tongue.

But I am encouraged by James' word, 'We *all* stumble in
many ways.' James was the brother of our Lord (Gal. 1:19),
or, being technical, half-brother. He was without question
the 'big gun' in the earliest church. His word was law, no
doubt because he was seen by all as Jesus' brother. In any

case, it is encouraging to me that he said what he did about not being perfect – that all of us, himself included, stumble in many ways.

James' opening statement in his discourse on the tongue therefore immediately disarms all of us, setting us free from unnecessary guilt, and thus lets us know that perfection, though we should regard it as a valiant goal, is not realistically expected by our gracious Heavenly Father. 'He remembers that we are dust' (Ps. 103:14). God does not want us to beat ourselves black and blue because we are not perfect. The best of God's servants in Scripture have had both successes and failures when it comes to tongue control. Only Jesus was perfect.

The word translated as 'stumble' in the NIV is from the Greek *ptaio*, which means 'to slip', 'to sin', 'to fall' or 'to offend'. James' point that 'whoever keeps the whole law and yet *stumbles* at just one point is guilty of breaking all of it' (Js 2:10) shows that he is talking about sin. Sinning with the tongue, however minute it may seem at first, has the potential to grieve the Holy Spirit seriously and cause unthinkable damage both to others and to ourselves.

We therefore have a mandate to deal with our tongues. The fact that we are not perfect and are not expected to be perfect is no warrant from God to settle for imperfection and to neglect this matter. As a matter of fact, we are warned in no uncertain terms of the grave consequences of not making every effort to control our tongues. We are fools if we do not take the word of God seriously and apply James' teaching to our lives.

As 1 Corinthians 13 is known as the 'love ' chapter of the Bible, Hebrews 11 being the 'faith' chapter of the Bible, so is James 3 the 'tongue' chapter of the Bible. We need to look carefully at what the Holy Spirit has to say throughout the Bible generally and especially through him.

However, I want us also to look at other Scriptures that deal with this subject as firmly as James did. What follows is so important that, just maybe, it could save lives – marriages, jobs, ministries, relationships and careers. It would not surprise me to learn that this came to you in the nick of time.

# 12

# The Tongue on the Way to Church

Save me, O Lord, from lying lips and from deceitful tongues. What will he do to you, and what more besides, O deceitful tongue?

*Ps. 120:2–3*

These words are from the first Psalm of Ascent. I have often wondered why, right at the beginning of this section (Ps. 120–134), we are given this word about the *tongue*. In a sense it is rather strange. Why would the psalmist plunge into this kind of subject when the ancient people of God were on their way to worship God in Jerusalem?

The Psalms of Ascent were sung by ancient Israelite pilgrims three times a year. They were sung on their way *up* to the three feasts of Jerusalem which they were required to attend. The word 'ascent' comes from the Hebrew word that means *going up*. I have written a book called *Higher Ground*, which deals with the fifteen Psalms of Ascent. No matter where the ancient Israelites journeyed from, they had to go *up to Jerusalem* because this amazing city is 2500 feet above sea level.

This psalm is about God getting our attention. What does God have to do to get our attention – even your attention? The funny thing is, the very thing that tends to put us off God is the very thing he uses to bring us back to him!

The psalm may be seen as one that the pilgrims sang when they realised what they needed before they could worship God properly. God had to bring distress to get their attention. 'I call on the Lord in my distress, and he answers me' (Ps. 120:1). God uses adversity – or whatever causes distress – to get our attention. It drives us to our knees. God does what he has to do to get us to call on him as we should.

I love the way the King James Version quotes Jonah 2:1: 'Then Jonah prayed.' The previous verse says that the Lord provided a great fish to swallow Jonah, that he was inside the fish three days and three nights, '*then* Jonah prayed'. And oh how he prayed!

What does it take to get you to pray? By the way, how much do you pray? How much time do you spend in prayer? Children spell 'love' T-I-M-E. What if God measures our love for him by how much time we have for him?

The first line in the first of the Psalms of Ascent therefore refers to calling on the Lord in distress. Perhaps it was distress that catapulted the pilgrims into making the journey up to Jerusalem. Maybe they did not want to go. They called on the Lord in distress, and he answered! And so now they are on their way up to Jerusalem in obedience to God's word.

It is much like going to church. God wants his people never to forsake the assembling of themselves together (Heb. 10:25). The Hebrew Christians in the first century were discouraged and were getting out of the habit of meeting together. So likewise do we sometimes rebel at going to church. We think of various reasons not to go – and we feel quite right about it.

But God has a way of getting our attention and showing us we need to meet with his people. Louise and I attend a little church in Key Largo, Florida. In their weekly bulletin are these words: 'Our Church Family is a group of imperfect people who have been brought together by the grace of God to worship him, to be reminded of his forgiveness and to find out what he wants us to do in this world.'

The Christian isn't perfect; no church is perfect. But we need to be there. But have you noticed how – at home beforehand and on the way to church – *the tongue* makes an attempt to spoil the whole thing? There is shouting, arguing, bickering, murmuring, defensiveness and the pointing of the finger – have you noticed it? Well, you are not alone. It is so typical and so frequent. *Satan does not want you to go to church.* He knows how to attack and to get us frustrated and angry at the very time we ought to be worshipful and full of anticipation.

Could this be why the psalmist mentions the tongue right at the beginning of the Psalms of Ascent? Take, for example, people coming from Galilee. It was a three-day journey. Today I drive it in three hours. But not then. And when a group of people are going to be living close together for three days, all kinds of tensions can set in. They begin annoying each other. Perhaps this is why the tongue is put right at the beginning of these psalms.

One form of distress God uses to get our attention is caused by the deceit of others. The origin of the psalmist's distress appears to be that he was criticised unfairly. That is enough to divert you from worshipping God. Criticism is painful, even if it is true. If a person begins a sentence, 'I say this in love' – watch out! But the psalmist was the victim of a deceitful tongue.

The psalmist had either been lied *to* or lied *about*. What is a lie? It is the postponement of the truth that will eventually come out. It is only a matter of time before the truth will come out. I guarantee it.

So relax. Lower your voice. Leave the lies to God. 'It is mine to avenge; I will repay,' says the Lord (Rom. 12:19). But it is still disconcerting when a lie is used by the devil to direct your attention away from God. It is equally true that God uses all this to get our attention so we will turn to him as we should.

In any case, on our way to worship the devil loves to use lies and deceit.

Bad things often happen when something good is supposed to happen – or is about to happen. Worshipping God is always good and right. We therefore should not be surprised when the devil enters the picture. And what is his instrument? Surprise, surprise. It is the tongue. The devil can do nothing without God's permission. God allows the devil to go so far, but no further.

When you are lied about it is a great opportunity for strength of character. You tell what you are when you are under fire. And there is nothing so intense as the heat of a deceitful or lying tongue. My advice (if you can take it): do not respond, focus on worshipping God. Keep going up to Jerusalem, go on to church. Get there and worship there.

In another psalm, David, when worshipping God and praying that his prayer be set before the Lord like incense, said: 'Set a guard over my mouth, O Lord; keep watch over the door of my lips' (Ps. 141:3).

One of my favourite places to eat in London was a Middle-Eastern restaurant. I went there so often that the chef once offered to prepare a special dish, noting that I love garlic. He took a large tomato, cut it several ways, then put a truckload of garlic and onions in the tomato, soaking in oil and vinegar, and let it set for fifteen minutes. It was indescribably delicious. When I arrived home, Louise said, 'What on earth have you eaten?' I explained. But all night long she kept asking me to roll over and face the other direction. The next morning I brushed my teeth, gargled and did everything I could to get the odour off my breath. Nothing worked. Wherever I went I did my best to keep my lips sealed rather than knock people over with my bad breath.

It taught me a lesson. When tempted to speak, always *think garlic*. It helps me to keep my mouth shut. I am reminded of those haunting words, 'When words are many, sin is not absent, but he who holds his tongue is wise' (Prov. 10:19).

It's a good thing to remember on the way to church. Or anywhere else.

## 13

# Asking for Trouble

Not many of you should presume to be teachers, my
brothers, because you know that we who teach will be
judged more strictly.

*Js 3:1*

Long before I felt the definite call of God on my life to be
a preacher it was drummed into me, 'Don't do it unless you
are called by God.' I don't know whether my old pastor
knew about Spurgeon's warning – 'If you can do anything
else, do it,' but I do know I was told that the ministry was
not for everybody, only those truly called by God.

Whereas Paul said that if anyone aspires to be a bishop, or
overseer, he desires a 'noble task' ('good work' – 1 Tim. 3:1,
KJV), James clearly puts obstacles in the way of anyone who
is thinking along the lines of going into the ministry.

If you wonder why James refers to being a 'teacher' rather
than 'preacher' it is because every preacher was supposed to

be a teacher. You might make a distinction between the two, which I could do, but the main thing to remember is that we who have the responsibility of dealing with God's word – whether we be evangelists, pastors, prophets or preachers – are expected to know what we believe and know how to make it clear to those who are under our leadership. Any high profile position among the people of God means that you are going to be judged by a different standard than others. Unfair? That is the way it is.

Some aspire to the ministry because they see it as glamorous. Some think it is prestigious. Others go into it because they can't find a good job doing anything else. I think of George Bernard Shaw's famous words, 'Those who can, do; those who can't, teach.'

In seventeenth-century England the best minds chose the ministry. This is not only because Oxford and Cambridge were originally set up when *theology reigned* but also because the minister was to be very highly educated – the people expected it. When you examine the ministers, vicars and priests who became clergy in the Church of England you find they were the 'top of the line'. Today many of the best minds seem to go into areas of study like physics, medicine or science. One should pray that this would change, that the most able people would want to go into the preaching or teaching ministry – that the church would be led by the most brilliant people.

But on one inflexible condition: that they are called by the Holy Spirit. One of the worst things that can happen to a person is to enter into the preaching or teaching ministry and not be called of God. It is a sure recipe for burnout and an eventual change of career. Most people who sit in the pews have no idea what it is like to be in the full-time ministry. It ain't all fun, I can tell you, and the only thing that keeps a person sane who is in this kind of calling is knowing that God put him or her there.

Perhaps you know about *The Peter Principle* by Laurence J. Peter; the thesis being that every person is promoted to the level of their incompetence. That may be true, but it is reassuring to know that the Holy Spirit never promotes us to the level of our incompetence. 'As thy days, so shall thy strength be' (Deut. 33:25, KJV). God will not lead you to do what you can't do. Just be sure you are being led by God himself!

James gives a sobering but sensible reason for avoiding the ministry, if you can: those who are in it will be *judged more strictly*. What does this mean? It basically means that those who are in the teaching or preaching ministry – whatever gives one a higher profile with the people of God – will not get away with lack of tongue control to the degree that others might do. As Dr O. S. Hawkins says, 'Teachers will be judged more strictly if their works do not match their words' (*Getting Down to Brass Tacks*, Loizeau Bros., p. 93).

This is for two reasons: (1) the people will judge you more harshly, and (2) God requires more of you. Regarding the first, once you are called into Christian ministry, like it or not, you are put on a pedestal in the eyes of the people. People will perceive you differently and consequently expect better behaviour – with particular reference to the tongue. You may say 'I am no different than others.' True; but you are *expected* to be different. 'That's not fair,' you may say. James' reply to you would be: don't even *think* about the teaching or preaching ministry if you feel that's unfair. You are not qualified. You are asking for trouble if you intend to be in the ministry. Once you accept the call of God on your life you must accept this matter as a 'given' – that people will always view you differently.

I was called into the ministry when I was 19 years old. Three months later I was called to be the pastor of the Church of the Nazarene in Palmer, Tennessee. I was startled to realise that these people were actually taking me seriously! I rather thought they might say, 'Oh, isn't he sweet' and overlook my youth and inexperience. But no. I was their pastor. They listened to what I said – in and out of the pulpit. I fear I failed many times in this area. God was gracious and patient with me. And so were some of them. But not all. One year later, when 'recall' time came, I scraped through with one vote enough to stay on. But I soon resigned, I was not ready for that – then.

But what is far more serious is the fact that God himself judges us more strictly. He clamps down on us in areas where he is not so hard with others. This may not bless you, but he seems to let the people of God generally get away with more than we in the ministry can get away with. Unfair? Sorry about that – that is the way it is. He may give them – to use an expression every golfer understands – a handicap. But not us!

God disciplines more strictly, judges more harshly, observes more carefully and scrutinises more often all those who accept his call to enter into the teaching or preaching ministry. This is what he does here below, and it says nothing about being judged at the Judgement Seat of Christ. We who are in the ministry are being dealt with here below day and night – all the time – on this earth. But when we stand before God at the Final Judgement we will find that there, too, we will be judged more strictly. To put it another way, it will be somewhat harder for us to get a reward at the

Judgement Seat of Christ than for those not in the ministry.

This should sober anybody who is thinking about going into the ministry. If you are not called by the Holy Spirit, you really are asking for trouble to pursue the ministry. Stay away from it!

# 14

# The Proof of Self-control

If anyone can control his tongue, it proves that he has
perfect control over himself in every other way.

*Js 3:2, LB*

A fruit of the Spirit is 'self-control' along with love, joy,
peace, patience and other virtues. Self-control sometimes
gets lost in this list of the fruits of the Spirit. When you stop
and think about it, it is an extraordinary virtue. Surely one
of the primary things that separates a Christian from a non-
Christian is that we have self-control. We are not mastered
by any sin!

But what is the proof that we have this self-control? Is it
because we are not addicted to alcohol, tobacco, sex,
pornography, drugs or excessive eating? Some may say that
our not being a slave to these proves that we have self-
control. This is true – up to a point. But according to James
the proof of self-control is that we control our tongues.

The Greek literally reads, as in the KJV: 'If any offend not in word, the same is a perfect man, and able to bridle the whole body.' The offence in word does not refer to sound or perfect doctrine, although we should aspire to this. He is talking about overcoming a loose tongue, unguarded and needlessly offensive comments. By 'whole body' he is not saying that tongue control will heal the body; he is talking about 'every other part of his personality' (Phillips Modern English).

The truth is, James did not introduce the subject of the tongue in James 3 but early on in this wonderful epistle. For example, the first impulse we often have when we are tempted is to say, 'I am tempted of God' or 'God is tempting me.' One must begin control of the tongue in the presence of God – and never accuse the Lord of tempting us because God 'cannot be tempted by evil, nor does he tempt anyone' (Js 1:13). Strength of character is refusing to say what you might think or feel, when you know in your heart that saying it will make things worse. Hence James gave that famous axiom, 'Everyone should be quick to listen, slow to speak and slow to become angry' (Js 1:19).

The tongue is the indicator of the heart. Out of the abundance of the heart the mouth speaks (Matt. 12:34). But you may reply, 'Then one automatically says what is on his heart – if you think it, do it.' Wrong. That is the devil speaking. What is on your heart may be right and good; it could be very wrong and evil. Tongue control is to discern your heart with objectivity so that you do not say what the devil would have you say.

There is a difference between temptation and sin. It is not a sin to be tempted; it is not a sin to have the thought. The sin is in our *words* – when we say what is tempting us. The temptation could be to lust or self-exaltation, name dropping or speaking ungraciously. The temptation to say such things is not sin; it is sin when we cave in to the temptation to cause another to lust, to say what makes us look good or to say what will make another look bad. Tongue control indicates whether the temptation was aborted and sin did not come forth.

The tongue therefore proves whether you are in control of your whole being. That is the fruit of the Spirit – self-control. The perfect man or woman therefore is not the one who doesn't have evil thoughts or wrong feelings; perfection is buttoning your lip so you do not say what you feel like saying. When we say what we feel in such circumstances it make things worse. This is why James says that the tongue is a 'small spark' that becomes a fire which can spread and do unthinkable damage (Js 3:5–6).

The perfect man or woman is the one who can 'bridle' his entire personality. The tongue therefore is not seen by James in these lines as a positive thing but a negative one. The tongue has no ability to come up with the right answer, no gift automatically to produce fruit. The function of the tongue in the Christian life is to abort temptation by refusing to speak. James is suggesting to us that if we will take care of the negative – by bridling the tongue – God will take care of the positive, speaking as the Holy Spirit would have us do.

James continues: 'When we put bits into the mouths of horses to make them obey us, we can turn the whole animal' (Js 3:3). As O. S. Hawkins says, 'No horse has ever bridled himself. Its master must do that. Likewise, try as we may, we cannot bridle ourselves. We need to yield our speech to the Master's control in order to receive direction in life. The bridle under a master's control benefits the horse by making him productive and leading him down the right path. Similarly, allowing the Master to control our tongues is for our own good' (*op. cit.*, p. 94).

I want to talk about tongues – the gift of tongues. Some sectors of the church emphasise the fruits of the Spirit to the neglect of the gifts; other movements of the church stress the gifts of the Spirit to the neglect of the fruits of the Spirit. To those who speak in tongues, one wants to ask: does speaking in tongues help you control your tongue? If speaking in tongues brought tongue control, it would be a tremendous testimony to the gift of tongues. But to my knowledge, alas, there does not seem to be a great correlation between speaking in tongues and controlling the tongue. I don't mean to be unfair, but I fear there are those who are intense about *speaking* in tongues and have not developed *control* of their tongues – that is, speaking in love and never pointing the finger or giving in to gossip.

This is not to be hard on those who speak in tongues. I speak in tongues. But I have to confess that speaking in tongues so far (I have been doing it for many years) has not given me great conscious help in tongue control. I find that my gift of tongues sometimes works without the fruit of the Spirit manifesting simultaneously. This is because the gifts are without repentance – that is, they are irrevocable (Rom. 11:29). This means that speaking in tongues is no sign of true spirituality. As a matter of fact, you can have the gifts of the Spirit and not be a spiritual person. King Saul prophesied (one of the gifts of the Spirit – see 1 Cor. 12:8–10) while he was on his way to kill David (1 Sam. 19:18–24).

What is even sadder is that there are those who emphasise the gift of tongues so much that they tend to judge people who do not speak in tongues as being less spiritual. Indeed, there are those who stress speaking in tongues with such vigour that they sometimes seem more anxious to get people to speak in tongues than they care about saving the lost. They become 'evangelistic' regarding the gift of tongues – and get heated sometimes when people disagree with them.

I say this lovingly, as I know people who speak in tongues but do not seem to have tongue control. It is not a good testimony for the gifts of the Spirit when we are deficient in the fruits of the Spirit. And one of the fruits of the Spirit is self-control! According to James, you do not have genuine self-control until you are able to control the tongue. It is the fruit of the Spirit that is relevant here. If we want the gifts of the Spirit to be enticing to those who are scared of them, we should hang our heads in shame if we do not have the fruits of the Spirit.

I take the view that there has been a silent divorce in the church, speaking generally, between the 'word' and the Spirit. When there is a divorce, sometimes the children stay with the mother, sometimes with the father. In this divorce between the 'word' and the Spirit, there are those on the 'word' side and those on the 'Spirit' side. Word people emphasise doctrine, expository preaching and upholding the faith once delivered to the church – and, yes, the *fruits* of the Spirit. Spirit people emphasise signs, wonders and miracles and the need to return to the Book of Acts – and, yes, the *gifts* of the Spirit.

What is needed today more than anything is not one or the other – but both! I personally suspect that the simultaneous combination would result in spontaneous combustion.

But any emphasis on the gifts without the fruits of the Spirit will be an unbalanced treatment of the New Testament and a gross example of being selective with God's infallible word. Therefore, speaking in tongues – the only gift of the Spirit that challenges our pride and therefore has the potential to keep one humble – will not be very attractive to those who try so hard to pursue the fruits of the Spirit – including control of the tongue. If we want people to desire our gifts we are duty bound to manifest self-control. According to James, the effort to control the tongue is the place to begin. But we will see that we have our work cut out for us!

# 15

# The Dangerous Potential
# of the Tongue

Consider what a great forest is set on fire by a small spark. The tongue also is a fire, a world of evil among the parts of the body.

*Js 3:5–6*

The tongue has the power of life and death.

*Prov. 18:21*

The tongue is a most extraordinary part of the body. By it we speak, send signals, feel and taste. It is unimaginable what life would be like without the tongue. I think of people who are not able to speak; what an inconvenience to lose the privilege of speaking or to be born without speech. Zachariah, the father of John the Baptist, was unable to speak for a period of time (Luke 1:20, 64). This was a temporary judgement inflicted upon him by the Spirit of God owing to his unbelief. How horrible it must have been for him in those days. And yet to live like this all the time is to experience much frustration.

The tongue is an instrument for incalculable good. By the tongue we praise God and sing to his glory. 'His praise was on my tongue' (Ps. 66:17). 'My tongue will tell of your righteous acts all day long' (Ps. 71:24). 'May my tongue sing of your word, for all your commands are righteous' (Ps. 119:172). 'Our mouths were filled with laughter, our tongues with songs of joy' (Ps. 126:2). By the tongue we spread the word of God. 'My tongue will speak of your righteousness' (Ps. 35:28). The tongue is the instrument of good teaching. 'My tongue is the pen of a skilful writer' (Ps. 45:1). 'The Sovereign Lord has given me an instructed tongue, to know the word that sustains the weary' (Isa. 50:4). It is the tongue that will one day proclaim the glory of Jesus Christ throughout the universe: because 'every tongue shall confess that Jesus Christ is Lord, to the glory of God the Father' (Phil. 2:11).

But did you know how little 'good' the tongue is said actually to do when you check the references to it in the Bible? I was amazed. The word 'tongue' is found in the Bible no fewer than 130 times. Except where it means language, the word tongue is seen as largely negative or potentially damaging in most places. I had to search diligently to get the positive quotations above! But consider for example these typical words:

You will be protected from the lash of the tongue. (Job 5:21)

With their tongue they speak deceit. (Ps. 5:9)

Trouble and evil are under his tongue. (Ps. 10:7)

Keep your tongue from evil. (Ps. 34:13)

I will watch my ways and keep my tongue from sin. (Ps. 39:1)

Your tongue plots destruction . . . like a sharpened razor. (Ps. 52:2)

A lying tongue hates those it hurts. (Prov. 26:28)

These are but a few verses, and I did not include above the many references to 'mouth', 'word', 'words' or 'lips', where you read equivalent descriptions that are mostly negative.

Yes, the potential for good is unlimited. 'A word aptly spoken is like apples of gold in settings of silver' (Prov. 25:11). Indeed, a word that is uttered even with no emotion or much volume can accomplish what no one had dreamed, as when a 'gentle tongue can break a bone' (Prov. 25:15). I watched with amazement when a cabinet minister in the British Parliament in one stroke brought down the career of former Prime Minister Margaret Thatcher in a few moments with a calm voice.

A famous anecdote reveals how the boisterous and unprepared preacher had written to the side of his notes: 'weak point, shout here'. There are times when raising the voice is good and right, as when Peter preached to thousands on the day of Pentecost (Acts 2:14). But if one shouts and harangues with no substantial content, the speaker is like a mouth full of gravel and the result is an audience with empty heads and hearts.

James points out that we can in some ways get the advantage over nature or creation. For example, we make a horse obey us with a bridle. We can work with the wind and direct a ship's direction by a small rudder (Js 3:3–4). He then shows the damage the tongue – such a small member of the body – can do. We might expect him to say what we can do to get on top of things when it comes to tongue control. But he concludes that the tongue 'no man can tame' (Js 3:8). Nobody can. Not a single person under heaven. Old or young. Rich or poor. No matter one's colour, race or nationality. Tongue control cannot be attained by any gift we have, by any amount of education we receive or by the highest level of intellect. (Now that would be unfair – giving smarter people an advantage!) But a high IQ doesn't even help. More involvement in Christian service will not bring you one whit closer to tongue control. Mixing with the elite, being upwardly mobile, making more money – all these are of no value in achieving control of the tongue.

And now for what may seem very astonishing to you (I wish it weren't so), James does not even say that there is anything that even *God* promises to do for us if we meet certain conditions. You read correctly, not even God himself promises to step in and give us relief in connection with tongue control. There are no simple promises that 'if we do *this*, God will do *that*'. Not so with becoming a Christian. To attain salvation all we have to do is to meet a simple condition: believe in the Lord Jesus Christ and we will be saved. The Bible is full of promises, offered on the basis of meeting certain conditions.

James does not offer one single promise that if we meet a

certain condition, God will fix up the tongue. Now he did so regarding the promise of wisdom. He said that if we desire wisdom we should ask God for it – in faith. Faith without wavering meets the condition for getting wisdom (Js 1:5–6). Moreover, we are promised the crown of life if we persevere when tried (Js 1:12). He said later on in his letter that if we resist the devil (a condition), he will flee from us (the promise – Js 4:7). He added that if you meet the condition of drawing close to God he promises that 'he will come near you' (Js 4:8). So we know, therefore, that James promises a lot of good things in his mighty little epistle – attaching certain conditions, using or implying the word 'if '.

But he does not offer a single promise of tongue control if we do certain things. If only he had said, 'Pray more, and you will achieve tongue control.' I wish he had said, 'Read your Bible every day and you will master the tongue.' I would even welcome the challenge from him, 'Go on a forty-day fast and you will conquer your tongue.'

A colourful, widely used and powerful preacher in the Church of the Nazarene known as Uncle Buddy Robinson was speaking in my old church and gave an 'altar call' for people to come forward. A lady was kneeling and praying at the altar and apparently getting nowhere. Uncle Buddy asked, 'What is your problem?' She replied, 'I can't get my tongue on the altar.' Uncle Buddy said to her, 'Sister, I can't see what the problem is. Your tongue is only four inches long and this altar is thirty feet long – surely you can get your tongue on it.' Quite. If only.

One of James' very purposes and motives in these lines is to bring us to the place where we see there is no hope of bridling the tongue – if we are expecting God to do it.

Indeed, he wants us to see that there is no hope of taming the tongue until we accept that God *isn't going to do it* for us. Why? It is because as long as we think that God will somehow take over, we won't do the first thing about it!

Take the matter of lust, which is treated earlier in this epistle (Js 1:13–15). If you think that God is behind your being tempted, you will somehow expect him, not you, to be the one to eradicate or control that lust. You conclude, therefore, that you are not responsible for your lust – he is. Wrong. We all have to deal with our own lust – and never accuse God. Each of us is tempted when we are enticed by our own evil desire. We are complete fools if we don't deal with it.

James elaborates on the danger of the uncontrolled tongue in these lines (Js 3:3–8). When it comes to lust, he shows that the end is death if the process of being tempted is not aborted along the way (Js 1:15). When it comes to the tongue he shows the potential damage that can come from it when it is not controlled. The tongue is 'a small part of the body' – a fact everybody knows. But even a Christian can do great damage, he warns us, if the tongue is not controlled. Conversion did not conquer the tongue problem. There is not a promised work of grace – second, third, fourth, tenth or hundredth – that will root out the problem of the tongue.

As a forest fire is started by a small spark, the tongue 'also is a fire' and spreads evil to all parts of the body – and we could add, the body of Christ. It corrupts the 'whole person' but equally spreads rapidly through the people of God and causes disruption, disunity, degradation, defeat and despair. It happens in families, at work or wherever we are in the world.

Whatever is James' point if there is nothing we can do and there is nothing that God promises to do? Is he trying to demoralise us? No. It is a wake-up call to take responsibility for our words and deeds so that we will be consciously aware and able to improve. God made us in such a way that we do change by being warned and seeing the consequences. We do! We are more likely to change when we see the danger and results if we don't change.

So does this mean that we can control the tongue after all? I answer: when we are sufficiently warned and motivated, we will care not to grieve the Holy Spirit of God and make changes. It does not mean we are perfect. But we can still improve. It is with the help of God and our working at it. In the words of Oliver Cromwell, 'Trust God and keep your powder dry.' It is a co-operative effort that effects change and can save us from disaster.

Some may wish to say, 'Man can't tame the tongue, but God can.' Yes. He can indeed. But he probably won't. God can do a lot of thing. He can stop hurricanes. He can stop earthquakes. He can stop crime. I used to say at Westminster Chapel, 'Boys and girls, God can do your homework for you.' But he never did mine! God motivates us by a strong word of warning. We are so stupid to ignore his word. When sufficiently motivated we will begin to take care when it comes to our words. We will probably start dealing with the tongue when we realise God won't do it for us – or we have been vehemently awakened. Probably not before. However, this is what James is trying to do for us.

I used to prepare sermons in a certain hotel in central London. I had a place where I could be alone, where nobody knew me, and only my wife and one or two close friends knew where I was. I came to the hotel one day to park next to it, but noticed a huge 'X' that extended to the length of a car. Someone said it was for diplomatic people to use. I questioned that and parked there. When I came out a few hours later my car was missing. I rushed into the hotel to report my stolen car. But when asked where I parked it the manager pointed out that that space was for a diplomat and that I might try calling the police to see where my car was. I did. They had it. They had towed it to North London – an hour's drive away – where I headed with the help of an expensive taxi ride. I had to pay a fee to retrieve the car and then received a huge penalty fine in the mail a few weeks later. I can say one thing: it worked! I never parked there again. Was it God who helped me? Perhaps. Or was I sufficiently motivated not to park there? Yes.

That is the way the mind of James works in these verses. Not that controlling the tongue is as easy as avoiding an illegal parking place. But there are things we can and must do – if we are to improve our tongue control. We will not get to perfection. Sorry about that! But we can improve. The paradox of Christian perfection is to admit our imperfection but strive for perfection none the less. God likes that. It works. We can get better. Not perfect. Better.

## 16

# The Fire of Hell

The tongue also is a fire . . . and is itself set on fire by hell.

*Js 3:5–6*

The Lord disciplines those he loves.

*Heb. 12:6*

James is doing his best to give every Christian a wake-up call. I call it internal chastening – warning of serious consequences through the word. There are three levels of chastening, or disciplining: (1) internal, (2) external and (3) terminal. The word translated as 'chasten' (KJV) or 'discipline' (NIV) comes from the Greek *paideuo* – a word that means 'enforced learning'. It is when God teaches us a lesson in such a way that we are without excuse if we remain the same afterwards.

To put it another way, internal chastening is God's Plan A for securing our obedience to his word. Plan A comes through teaching, preaching, worshipping, fellowship, a slap on the wrist from a friend or wise counselling. Whenever God speaks to us without putting us flat on our backs to get our attention, we should welcome it. Plan A is the best way to get our problems solved. This happens when we hear him speak and we reply, 'Yes Lord' – and also prove it by a life of more careful obedience.

Then there is Plan B – external chastening. It is when God uses external force rather than the word. He may indeed put us on our backs. He may bring sickness, financial reverse, loss, exposure, the withholding of vindication, marriage breakdown or any number of things. It is when Plan A fails that God institutes Plan B – to get our attention. It too is a wake-up call but it is more painful. It is carried out by a loving Heavenly Father because we did not listen to him when he was carrying out Plan A.

The Epistle of James is Plan A. But in James 3:5–7 he *describes* what I am calling Plan B. He lets us see how bad it can get if we don't listen to his warning to deal with the tongue. He shows the horror that the unguarded comment can cause, what pointing the finger will do, what spreading gossip leads to, what sending people on a guilt grip ends up doing or what accusing God brings on. God steps in with Plan B because we did not take heed to the word.

God's Plan B can be pretty awful. Things happen that are so dreadful – it is called the fire of hell – that we would give a thousand worlds to turn the clock back so we could listen again to Plan A.

Plan C is carried out by God when even Plan B fails. It is the worst possible scenario for a true Christian. This is evidenced when either a person cannot be renewed again to repentance (Heb. 6:6) or when one commits the sin unto death (Acts 5:1–10; 1 Cor. 11:30; 1 John 5:16). If God bringing on external chastening doesn't wake us up so as truly to get our attention, we leave God with no choice but to judge us with terminal chastening – the final measure of disciplining. I have developed this more fully in *The Judgment Seat of Christ*.

The saddest thing in the world in this matter is that you cannot take back what you said. The careless word was a spark that started a forest fire. We may say 'sorry' and mean it, but the damage is done. 'An offended brother is more unyielding than a fortified city' (Prov. 18:19). We may cry out, 'I wish to God I hadn't said it,' but it is too late. The spark started the fire. All the water from the seven seas would not put out the fire.

In a courtroom a defence lawyer or prosecutor may lead a witness to say something that the judge overrules. The judge strikes it from the record and cautions the jury to disregard the comment. But everybody knows it was said and many don't forget it when they deliberate on a verdict. The overruled word often still rules and reigns.

I have known occasions when God mercifully, if not miraculously, stopped me from uttering something that would have been disastrous. I have also known occasions when Matthew 10:20 (about taking no thought what to say but letting the Holy Spirit speak through you) was in operation. Yes, sometimes in what I can only call an 'emergency situation' God may reach down and stop our mouths or control our tongues.

But the Christian life is to be lived generally in non-emergency conditions. We must not expect him to treat us as if we were in a life or death situation all the time, constantly rescuing us from ourselves and giving us perfect words. God does not work with us apart from the real world we live in. The sooner we accept this the sooner it will have an effect on the way we speak. James is wanting to help us avoid tragedies.

I don't know anybody who can read this section of James and feel good. It is disquieting, discomforting and sobering. If reading this does that for you, good. There is hope. James wants to box us in. If we get defensive, however, we may not learn anything from him. And yet it is far better to get angry with him – and still later take his warning on board – than to say, 'Yes Lord' and not change. Jesus' parable of the two sons is appropriate here.

> There was a man who had two sons. He went to the first and said, 'Son go and and work today in the vineyard.' 'I will not,' he answered, but later he changed his mind and went. Then the father went to the other son and said the same thing. He answered, 'I will, sir,' but he did not go. Which of the two did what his father wanted?' 'The first,' they answered.
>
> Matt. 21:28–31

In a word: if reading this book brings an immediate 'Yes Lord', that is good – so far. But the worst thing that can happen is to be instantly and immediately stirred then revert to your old ways. I would far prefer that you say 'No' and be upset, except that you are later granted repentance so you can be renewed again. This shows that Plan B is working and that you have not fallen into terminal chastening.

James' goal for us is that we – in ever-increasing measure – will experience the wisdom that comes from heaven that is pure, peace-loving, considerate, submissive, full of mercy and good fruit, impartial and sincere (Js 3:17). We get closer and closer to this goal by taking his words with utmost seriousness.

'A fool gives full vent to anger, but a wise person quietly holds it back' (Prov. 29:11, New Living Translation). Giving full vent to your anger is when the devil achieves his wish for you – that you lose your temper, shout and blame – and leave all around you scared and upset. That is when the fire of hell sweeps through your life and surroundings. The devil has a party in hell, as it were, drinking to his victory over you and to your defeat in controlling the tongue. My loving advice: *don't give Satan that pleasure*.

To be honest with you, if there has been some improvement in me over the years, it has been because God carried out Plan B in my life. More often than I want you to know. I know what it is to set a forest on fire by my uncontrolled words – to feel the very fire of hell, when the breath of Satan entered the room and won a big victory.

It is not a happy thought that the devil got in and orchestrated our words. But this has happened to me, and it can happen to you. When all hell breaks loose through our tongues it is because the tongue was set on fire by hell itself. The tongue is a fire that spreads evil throughout our entire personality. We lose control. We say things that would make the angels blush. We would die a thousand deaths if a video of ourselves were to be re-played before the world. It all happened because the devil entered in – through a spark – and won. Like a pilot light in a stove or an oven waiting to be ignited by gas, so the tongue just needs a spark to burst into flames.

The tongue therefore can be inflamed by hell. The tongue is not only what made hell necessary; hell itself ultimately lies behind tongues that spread deadly poison. It is the behind-the-scenes explanation for anger, lost tempers, contorted faces, wounded feelings, words that engender jealousy and fear. It is all because the tongue is itself set on fire by hell (the Greek word *gehenna* is the word actually used). *Gehenna* (used 12 times) is the principal word used in the New Testament for hell. *Gehenna* was the place where rubbish was burnt outside one of the city gates of Jerusalem. The fires of *gehenna* were always burning.

Jesus adopted this word *gehenna* for his teaching on everlasting punishment. And James uses it to connote the idea that Satan's future and final place of destiny – which exists now – somehow works its way into conversations when we are not sufficiently careful.

Why is the tongue called fire? Because it gets so easily out of control. Whatever it burns is destroyed and brought to complete disuse; what is burnt is never the same again. It is called fire because what we do to ourselves is damage, sometimes taking a good while to get things back together. The tongue is a ready and most co-operative weapon when the urge to speak – to 'put the record straight' or to have the last word – takes over. It is called fire because we so often do irreparable damage to others – even those closest to us.

Satan knows all about hell. It is the fire of hell that motivates the devil to work so violently. He knows where he is going to end up. He knows his time is short (Rev. 12:12). It is his knowledge of his impending doom that lies behind the violence that he does. He knows he is going to hell. The tongue is his best weapon to conserve the damage already done, and it is his best weapon to continue the spread of evil.

In a word: the devil is on the road to hell and wants, if

possible, to take as many with him as possible. He wants to create chaos in the meantime. He wants to inflame and paralyse Christians. He wants Christians to get burned by their words. He wants Christians to burn others by an ill choice of words. It happens in families, in marriages, in church meetings and business meetings, in deacons' meetings, in parking lots after the church service, in cars on the way to church.

*It* [the tongue] *represents among our members the world with all its wickedness; it pollutes our whole being; it keeps the wheel of our existence red-hot, and its* *flames are fed by hell.*

Js 3:6, New English Bible

Hell was created for the devil and his angels (Matt. 25:41). Satan fell by uttering threatening words such as 'I will be like God' (Isa. 14:14). The tongue brought about his own downfall. He has been seeking vengeance ever since by getting people to do what he did – and utter heinous and, if possible, blasphemous words. He wants to bring about our downfall and destroy all he can before he meets his own final doom. His anger towards God, his hatred towards righteousness, his ire towards every child of God and his wrath towards all that is good is so quickly displayed once we lose tongue control.

Poisonous words corrupt our whole person, says James. We are left demoralised, weakened, compromised, defeated and jaundiced. All is yellow to the jaundiced eye. We are angry with the world, our loved ones, our friends, our neighbours, ourselves. The dove – the Holy Spirit – lifts from us and flies away, leaving us to ourselves. We become unteachable, defensive, irritable, full of self-pity, full of unkindness. When we speak in that condition nothing comes out right.

This means sometimes that we are seriously backslidden. It does not mean that Plan C is the next thing God is going to put into operation. That would only happen if one did not wake up. Not waking up after so many forms of external chastenings – and seeing the fire of hell manifested before our eyes – is certainly not a good sign. But as long as you can feel truly remorseful and repentant, there is hope.

The proof that we are not in a terminal chastening mode is that we are given sorrow for sin. God grants unfeigned repentance. We confess it to him. When we do so he is faithful and just to forgive us our sins and to cleanse us from all unrighteousness (1 John 1:9). Not only are we granted the ability to repent, we are changed from glory to glory by the Holy Spirit (2 Cor. 3:18). As long as we enjoy being changed from glory to glory, it is not only a wonderful sign that we have not become stone deaf to the Spirit but that God is at work in us. Knowing this is a very good feeling.

Repentance (Gr. *metanoia* – 'change of mind') shows that we are still being changed. Despite our stupidity and folly, God stoops to our weakness to give us help. It shows he is not finished with us. The worst scenario, then, is to become stone deaf to the Spirit – that we hear nothing from him. But if the word of God convicts us, it means we are not stone deaf to his Spirit but are indeed hearing his voice. A wonderful feeling indeed.

So do not be discouraged if you have failed with the tongue. Do not be demoralised if you have flamed the fires of hell. Do not be in despair just because the devil celebrated a victory over you.

Why? Because the devil always overreaches himself. If

you will stand on God's word when you are put through the fire, you will see – in time – that what happened that was bad will still work together for good (Rom. 8:28).

> When thro' fiery trials thy pathway shall lie,
> My grace, all sufficient, shall be thy supply.
> The flames shall not hurt thee; I only design
> Thy dross to consume and thy gold to refine.
>
> *George Keith*

I believe I should tell you that I think I have made nearly every mistake that could be made when it comes to lack of tongue control. But God has been patient with me. Our Heavenly Father is a gracious God. I ought to know.

# 17

# Poison

No man can tame the tongue. It is a restless evil, full of
deadly poison.

*Js 3:8*

The tongue is not a neutral thing. It is a vile part of our
being and is – in and of itself – intrinsically evil, wicked and
poisonous. It is not our words that make the tongue deadly
poisonous; the tongue is already poisonous before we utter
a single word. This is because the tongue mirrors the heart.
Jesus said, 'Out of the heart come evil thoughts, murder,
adultery, sexual immorality, theft, false testimony, slander.'
This is Jesus' diagnosis of the heart of all men and women.
These startling words to the self-righteous Pharisees
followed his statement that 'the things that come *out of the
mouth* come from the heart' (Matt. 15:18–19).

Now you know where James got his teaching.

James contrasts the tongue with nature: 'All kinds of

animals, birds, reptiles, and creatures of the sea are being tamed and have been tamed by man, but no man can tame the tongue' (Js 3:7–8). Such living creatures are not guilty of deadly poisonous tongues.

Does this surprise you? Did you think that the tongue of a human being was a neutral member of our personality? Natural, yes, but not neutral.

Behind all that James teaches us – which he got straight from Jesus – is his robust doctrine of sin. We may not like it. We have seen the importance of a biblical doctrine of sin already in this book. It is a matter so often swept under the carpet. We are living in a day when the church, speaking generally, has such a superficial doctrine of sin that we should not be surprised about our lack of impact in the world. First, many have forgotten that we are *born* with a fallen nature. Second, many have also forgotten that we *retain* this fallen nature after conversion – and will have it until we see Jesus face to face (1 John 3:2). That is what theologians call glorification (Rom. 8:30).

It seems almost redundant to say it, but we are not glorified yet. We are still sinners. To recall Martin Luther's coined phrase, 'simultaneous saint and sinner', referring to every Christian; the holiest man or woman is still a sinner. This may not fit well with some people's doctrine of sanctification, but this is what Jesus taught, it is what Paul the Apostle taught and what James is telling us in these lines that are quite out of our comfort zone.

The tongue, he tells us, *is* (not was) 'a restless evil, full of deadly poison'. Furthermore, it does not become that; it is that. James is describing your tongue and mine. He is describing his own tongue, the Apostle John's tongue, Peter's tongue, Elijah's tongue, Daniel's tongue, Abraham's tongue,

Moses' tongue, King David's tongue. Only Jesus was born without sin and only Jesus lived without ever sinning (Heb. 4:15).

I was brought up to believe in 'sinless perfection' – or something very close to that. I was taught that a Christian does not sin because a Christian must live above sin. As for James' comment, 'we all stumble in many ways', they would say that stumbling is not necessarily sinning. They would call it 'mistake', 'error', 'fault' or anything other than *sin*. When I used to ask why did Jesus give us the Lord's Prayer that includes 'forgive us our trespasses' (sins) if he knew Christians could reach a state of grace that puts one beyond daily sinning, some would say that the prayer was given 'before Pentecost' – or give no answer at all.

Even if you did not have my background, I ask you: do you have a good understanding of sin – of the human heart, of what is true of all people?

My ministry over the past fifty years has crossed many denominational and theological lines. I have been blessed in this regard. I have been fortunate to minister to people of all theological, cultural, ethnic and church backgrounds. It is my observation that most Christians have a deficient doctrine of sin. A superficial understanding of sin will mean a shallow theology. J. I. Packer says that the Bible Belt is a thousand miles wide and one inch deep.

We are simply not happy to think that we are wicked inside. We like to think that our being saved – or being filled with the Spirit – moves us beyond having to see ourselves as 'vile', to use Augustus Toplady's word in his classic hymn 'Rock of Ages'.

Why is this so important? I answer: that we will not be shocked at ourselves when poison proceeds from our mouths. It is important to our sanity, our peace and our understanding of God and his word. Do not be surprised if you discover that to the degree you come to terms with the wickedness of your tongue and its potential for danger will be the degree to which you are motivated to control that tongue.

Holiness is achieved, little by little, not in proportion to our denying sin but in proportion to our coming to terms with its existence – in ourselves. 'If we claim to be without sin, we deceive ourselves and the truth is not in us' (1 John 1:8). These words should shake us rigid, as James' word about our tongues being a restless evil and full of deadly poison should do. James and John have the same doctrine of sin.

James does not write these words as if to say, 'Get rid of this condition – do something about it.' He does not pose a work of grace that will bring the tongue back to the pre-fallen state of human beings. The vile tongues we are born with are here to stay – that is, as long as we are in this world. If there were a work of grace that would enable one to put his or her tongue on the altar and then be totally delivered, ah – how nice and lovely!

Some want to deal with the problem through casting out demons – by exorcisms. If only. I wish. I have had some very sincere charismatic friends who tried to cast demons out of me. More than once. I can tell you, I want all the help I can get and I will go anywhere to get the final victory over the tongue in advance of glory. The problem is, I sometimes began to wonder (do forgive me for this) if those who wanted to cast out demons had demons themselves because they too seemed to have problems with tongue control; temper, pointing the finger, gossip and, in some cases, lust. Oh dear.

Don't get me wrong. I believe there are demons. I also believe in deliverance from demons. But not all problems are demonic. Making demons the explanation for all our maladies is often a cop-out in order to avoid rugged self-discipline.

We are better off believing James – and accepting what he says about the tongue. It is not a neutral member of the body. It mirrors the heart. The heart is the fountain of all the evil speaking we do.

Thank God for the blood of Jesus. As we walk in the light, as he is in the light, we have fellowship with him and his blood cleanses us from all sin (1 John 1:7). The cleansing is not eradicating sin or pulling it out by the roots; it is making us feel forgiven, giving us peace and enabling us to face our Heavenly Father knowing that he knows all about us and still loves us! The cleansing of the blood of Jesus is what gives us intimacy with the Father, joy in the Holy Spirit, the feeling of being totally forgiven. It comes as we walk in the light.

Part of walking in that light is accepting what James says about the tongue and then being sufficiently convicted that we want to do something about it. We can. There is more that we can do than we may want to admit.

Some people go from one extreme to the other. On the one hand they want to say that the tongue is a neutral thing – as if to say that we do not stumble in many ways. The other extreme is to say that God will control the tongue for us if we let him! James adopts neither view. The truth lies between these extremes. Our tongues are deadly poisonous; we can still improve and aim for perfection. The onus is on us to fight this battle, to get better and better at overcoming unguarded comments and to stop engaging in pointing the finger. We can all do more than we may want to concede.

The tongue is therefore not a neutral thing but is by nature leaning toward hell's pull. It waits for our lack of self-control to ignite the flame or spread its poison in order to give the devil a victory. The tongue is the official spokesperson for our fallen nature. Biblical theology teaches us that there is fallen nature (people) and unfallen nature (trees and animals). Although nature is affected by the fall, it is not properly said to be fallen. Nature is cursed due to the fall (Gen. 3:17), but there is nothing sinful about nature. 'All kinds of animals, birds, reptiles and creatures of the sea are being tamed and have been tamed by man' (Js 3:7). It is man – and woman – who is the culprit. The tongue is the immediate indicator of our motivation: our sexual urge, self-esteem and ambition.

The easiest and most natural thing in the world is to give in to the heart, whether it be to jealousy, sexual temptation, saying something unflattering about another, accusing and blaming people, or giving in to bitterness or fear. Lust is enflamed by the tongue. Jealousy increases by the tongue. Our defensiveness gets worse when the tongue gets involved. You try to get the last word and you lose control.

You say to yourself, 'I will feel better if I get this off my chest.' So you do it. You get it off your chest. Lo and behold, you *do* feel better. For a while. But only for a while. The poison you spouted did not rid the heart of that poison, it only let it settle for a short time. Like pornography, which plays into an insatiable appetite for lust, so the tongue saying what it feels like saying only lets the poison build up until the volcano erupts next time. 'The heart is deceitful above all things and beyond cure' (Jer. 17:9).

Our heart is an incurable part of fallen nature, says James.

All else in nature is tameable: animals, fish, reptiles, birds. Man was given dominion over all creatures – animals, birds, fish (Gen. 1:26, 28). The devil isn't interested in getting at beasts, fish or birds. A bird, a fish or a tree can't spread evil! Satan's natural enemy is man – all because we were created in God's image (Gen. 1:26). Satan hates *us* – not flowers, mountains, giraffes, groupers, dolphins, monkeys, dogs, cats or birds. Satan's arch-enemy is the Lord Jesus Christ. God hates him because he did not take on the nature of angels but the seed of Abraham (Heb. 2:16, KJV). God was made *flesh* (John 1:14). That's us! All that Satan can do to man is an attack on Jesus Christ.

To put it another way: Satan is jealous of us. He cannot be redeemed, but we can. He cannot be saved, but we can. He cannot improve, but we can. He hates the Saviour of the world who came to save people. The devil is jealous of Jesus Christ, therefore hates us who are his brothers and sisters (Heb. 2:11).

What Satan feels towards us is best expressed by the word *poison*. Deadly poison. Poison destroys. So in order to inflict injury on the body of Jesus Christ the devil appeals to our fallen nature to say poisonous things – to make others feel bad and look bad. He feels that way already but he cannot get that across without our help. Our poisonous tongues oblige.

Do you realise what a high privilege it is to be made in the image of God? Satan hates us because we resemble God. Do you realise what a wonderful privilege it is to be called sons of God? The devil hates us because we resemble Jesus Christ. Do you realise what an honour it is for us to participate in the cosmic war between Christ and Satan? We will one day participate in his everlasting downfall. He knows that and hates us for it. But we will be praising God throughout eternity for this privilege.

Thus, to the extent we learn to be slow in speaking and quick in listening we will be less likely to manifest wrath. I say to you and to myself: let us not give the devil an inch. Let us beware that our poisonous tongues are vulnerable and overly willing to co-operate with his evil suggestions – especially if we have an enemy or if we have been deeply hurt by somebody. Or are jealous of another. The devil has a computer printout on our personalities, strengths, weaknesses, hurts, liabilities, enemies and friends. He is extremely clever. My dad used to say to me when I was a little boy, 'Son, the devil is crafty and second only to God in wisdom and power.' But he is second – not equal!

'Resist the devil, and he will flee from you,' says James (4:7). It is part of being spiritual to know the devil's ways. Paul said, 'We are not ignorant of his devices' (2 Cor. 2:11, KJV). I do not mean we should concentrate on being experts regarding the devil. Those who spend their time trying to understand the devil more than they do getting to know God will inevitably fall like pancakes. And yet we should know Satan's ways and therefore realise how he plays on our hurts and jealousies, our weaknesses and our pride. That is why we love gossip – the fodder for grieving the Holy Spirit.

Because the tongue is poison we drink this deadly poison when the tongue is uncontrolled. We take poison into our beings when we say or repeat unkind things *about* people, when we say things *to* people that make them feel inferior, when we are not gracious and when we speak out of fear. So if you and I do these things we are not only spreading poison, we are drinking it. It is almost like committing spiritual suicide. Poison will either kill you or make you deathly ill. Speaking without thinking is tantamount to swallowing deadly poison.

How do we poison others? First, by what we say without graciousness to people directly. It does not matter how old they are or how young, how educated or uneducated, how cultured or uncultured, whether they are saved or lost, whether their ethnic background is red, yellow, black or white. As Mark Twain said, 'Kindness is the language which the deaf can hear and the blind can see.'

Never assume that people will react to what you say with indifference. You may speak curtly to them and think they are thick-skinned and won't mind it. You are almost certainly wrong. People who appear to be thick-skinned happen to be among the most sensitive and emotional people of all. They cry inside but would never show it to you. What is more, when you hurt people you grieve the Holy Spirit. And never assume a person is so full of grace that they can cope with your harsh words. Even Jesus was affected by what people said; he simply could handle it without sinning (Heb. 4:15).

When we speak without thinking to others we may put temptation in their way and possibly even lead them to sin. Your words could speak fear into them. You could destroy them. This is why James calls the tongue deadly poison.

Secondly, we poison others by what we say to them about others. We could easily damage the person we are talking to; they may be crushed by what they hear from us. They may have a very high opinion of someone. They may hold a leader in high esteem. They may deeply respect another Christian. When they hear from us that so-and-so is not perfect (or whatever) it could wound the spirit of the person we tell this to. They may never get over it. In the process we may destroy another's reputation. We thus grieve the Holy Spirit.

What you say about others will almost certainly not be forgotten. You are responsible for shaping that person's opinion of others. They may never be able to feel the same way about that person – and you have this matter on your hands for life.

Always assume that what you say will be quoted. If you don't want it repeated, don't say it – ever, to anybody. How will you feel if what you say about a person gets back to that same man or woman? When it is quoted it will continue to have a detrimental effect. Once a person learns what you said, they may never recover. The tongue is poison. Don't be like the person who once said to me, 'I promised I wouldn't repeat this so listen carefully – I can only tell it once.'

Keep in mind that James is speaking like this so that: (1) we will see that God isn't going to tie down our tongues; (2) we will mourn for our sin and be ashamed for the hurts we have caused in the past – and repent; and (3) we will see how damaging our words are to others. Seeing these things and being convicted by the Holy Spirit is what will enable us – with his help – to get closer to tongue control.

# Part Four
# Motivation to Change

The purpose of James' epistle is to change lives. It was written to Jewish Christians, probably in Jerusalem and possibly well before AD 50. It could be the earliest epistle in the New Testament. The early Christians of Jerusalem needed to be jolted. They had begun taking themselves too seriously, forgetting the poor and wanting to appeal to the more prestigious Jews (see Js 2). Their lack of tongue control caused serious divisions in this early church. But it could not be more relevant for us in the twenty-first century.

How do you motivate people to change, especially when perfection should be our aim and yet knowing at the same time it is not an achievable goal?

I am a perfectionist. I have been this as far back as I can remember. I was driven by a strong father who wanted me to achieve. Making Bs in school when I was young was not good enough. I was urged to make As, not even A minuses! My church background, teaching 'Christian perfection' as they did, only added to my problem. I realise that many readers may not have this problem, but I think this might be helpful to some and also enable you to see where I am coming from.

My own dilemma therefore has been this. When I set a goal for myself I want to feel it is reachable and that I can and will accomplish it. If it is an unrealistic goal I tend to give up from the start. So when I know that I am not going to realise perfect tongue control while I am on this planet, I tend to say 'what's the use?' Therefore, it has been a major step forward for me to set out to achieve what is not achievable, namely, controlling the tongue and never stumbling by my senseless comments.

So why have I made this step? Two reasons. First, I have been boxed in by my loving Heavenly Father. I have made so many embarrassing mistakes that God has, as it were, put a pistol to my head to *change my manner of conversation*. It is as though the Lord has said, 'R.T., either change – or else.' Secondly, our ultimate goal in life should be to please God. I hope I don't sound pious in saying that, but that is the way it is. We should have a desire that goes from the crown of our heads to the soles of our feet and to our fingertips to please God. God, by his grace, wants us to be like that. It is his grace that will give us that. Therefore, we should want to pursue control of the tongue while accepting that we will only make measured, or limited, progress. But knowing that this pursuit truly pleases God is good enough for me!

I have prayed hard about this book. I have prayed hard to write in a manner that will help motivate the reader to want to change as we move closer to the conclusion of the book.

# 18

# Scandalous Worship

> With the same tongue we praise our Lord and Father, and
> with it we curse men . . . Out of the same mouth come
> praise and cursing.
>
> *Js 3:9–10*

God inhabits the praises of his people (Ps. 22:3, KJV). The
more we see this the more we will want to worship God,
whether it be in private devotional time or in public
worship with lots of singing. Our worship honours God and
also brings about blessing to us for doing it (see Ps. 67:5–6).
I would say this is true even if our worship is partly in the
flesh, partly in the Spirit.

No worship here below will be perfect. Even on Palm
Sunday when the multitudes of the people were shouting
'Hosanna!' we learn that their worship was very selfishly
motivated. But Jesus affirmed it all, knowing full well that
they were thinking one thing (Jesus was going to overthrow

Rome) and he was thinking something else (that he would go to the cross). Praising God for the wrong reasons is still mercifully accepted by God. And yet we wish for 'a thousand tongues to sing my great Redeemer's praise', as Charles Wesley put it.

There are levels of imperfection in worship, and what James talks about here really gets close to the bone. When he speaks of praising God and cursing men in the same breath I think of the following:

1  Going to church when you have been saying uncomplimentary things about the same church or its leader.
2  Worshipping God when you are angry they are not singing a song or hymn you know – or like.
3  Reading your Bible and trying to pray when you are in the middle of an argument with your spouse.
4  Holding a grudge towards your enemy and feeling no shame as you are singing the praises of God.
5  Speaking in an unflattering way about the same people who sit near you in worship.
6  Singing hymns while feeling jealous about the accomplishments of the person who sits next to you.
7  Praying and looking at your watch as you contemplate how you need to get away.
8  Listening to the sermon and thinking about how someone else there is the one who really needs this.
9  Asking God to bless you through the word when you are preoccupied with those you have spoken against.
10  Entering the service with anger from a conversation that just took place – which is unfinished – and thinking of what you will say all through the service rather than worshipping and listening to God.

11 Sitting in church – or at home in your quiet time – feeling no shame over how you have been entering into gossip.

12 Expressing your love to God when you in fact speak ill of some who are his children and your brothers and sisters.

13 Worshipping God in church when you would be embarrassed for those in the workplace to see you because you don't practise what you preach.

14 Taking responsibility in church when members of your family are either neglected or question the sincerity of your devotion.

15 Being faithful in church attendance when you neglect duties in the home.

16 Having your neighbours see you faithfully going to church while you have a poor testimony with them.

17 Showing a bad attitude in traffic on the way to church, then participating in worship with no apparent need to repent.

18 Meditating upon God's word without any sense of shame when you have just vehemently pointed the finger at someone.

19 Praying for the poor of this world when you avoid them after the service is over.

20 Thanking God for the blood of Jesus washing away your guilt while you have been an expert in sending people on guilt trips.

The list could be endless. I came up with many of the above examples because they describe me more often than I dare think about.

James says that 'this should not be' (Js 3:10). True, no

doubt. But that is the way it is. But if you and I aspire to a greater measure of the Holy Spirit and want to experience the 'wisdom that comes from heaven', there need to be some major changes in our lives. We begin with the tongue.

A young preacher asked me recently if I had any advice for him. I replied, 'Find out what grieves the Holy Spirit and don't do that.'

The teaching that I have developed over the years that has been the greatest motivating force to improve my personal life is in the matter of grieving the Holy Spirit. I have dealt with this in considerable detail in *The Sensitivity of the Spirit*. Here are some things I have learned about the Third Person of the Godhead:

1   The Holy Spirit is a very sensitive person. I don't really think it is possible to exaggerate how easy it is to grieve the Holy Spirit. 'Do not grieve the Holy Spirit of God, with whom you were sealed for the day of redemption' (Eph. 4:30). The word translated 'grieve' means to get your feelings hurt. Like it or not, the Holy Spirit is a highly sensitive person who gets his feelings hurt – very easily. Like a dove, a very shy bird that cannot bear noise and tension, the Holy Spirit lifts and flies away when we grieve him. This leaves us to ourselves, usually irritable and unable to think clearly, having forfeited presence of mind.

2   We almost never know it at the exact moment when we actually grieve the Spirit. The departing dove does not bring down thunder and lightning, he just unobtrusively flutters away – and we find later that we grieved him. Like Samson who did not know the Lord

had departed from him (Judg. 16:20), so we carry on as if nothing happened.

3   The chief way we grieve the Spirit is by bitterness. 'Get rid all bitterness, rage and anger, brawling and slander, along with every form of malice' (Eph. 4:31). We betray our bitterness by the way we speak to people and about people.

4   The Holy Spirit is no respecter of persons and will not bend the rules for any of us – whether we are church leaders with a high profile, veteran Christians, we pray two hours a day, are deacons or are counted as worthy saints by all believers. Those who enter into conversation that Jesus would not enter into grieve the Spirit.

This brings up that ugly word, gossip. I hate the word. It is what sells millions of cheap and tawdry magazines that are in your face as you check out of a supermarket. I so despise them that I like to think I am above this stuff. I may not read these magazines, but I am just as guilty as those who do read them when I myself hear with glee that a person I don't like has been found out – and I pass it on; or I repeat news of something unflattering about an enemy or a person who has wanted to hurt me in some way; or I make a person feel good whom I know would relish news of their enemy's difficulty. When I enter into conversations like this, *I grieve the Holy Spirit.*

Gossip is a defence mechanism to preserve our self-esteem. It arises out of an inferiority complex; we build ourselves up by tearing others down – or enjoying hearing that they are in trouble of some kind. It is a poisonous habit, which betrays our insecurity and lack of spirituality. If gossip makes us feel better we are self-deceived.

We may claim to be Spirit-filled, sound in our theology, faithful in our commitment to the church, zealous in worship and have devotional lives that are highly admirable. But when we grieve the Spirit by bitterness, expressions that expose our envy and jealousy, or saying what comes to mind that is not honouring to God, we become the very examples James laments: we praise the Lord and curse men.

He asks, 'How can fresh water and salt water flow from the same spring?' (Js 3:11). If the well in us – the Holy Spirit (John 7:38–39) – overflows, one expects the fruits of the Spirit such as love, joy, peace, patience, etc. (Gal. 5:22). But when the Spirit begins to speak and suddenly there emerges harshness, anger, vengeance and envy, something has gone terribly wrong.

This can happen when one preaches – apparently under the anointing – and then throws in a personal word that is aimed at someone in the congregation whom the speaker thinks needs to be sorted out. It can happen when one prays aloud – and then goes to moralising others in the same prayer. It is when one lays hands on people to be blessed – but speaks out against those who may not agree with the practice. Worst of all, it does not appear in the slightest to bother those who do it.

We have noted that the gifts are without repentance and are irrevocable (Rom. 11:29). Strange as it may seem, a person's gift may continue to flourish while the dove flies away! This is because you don't necessarily need the fruits of the Spirit for the gifts to function. Grieving the Spirit pertains more to the fruits – love, joy, peace – than to the gifts of the Spirit.

What motivates me to improve is that I do not want to grieve the Holy Spirit. Not because I fear I will lose my salvation or my gift; I am so afraid of losing the anointing. I know exactly what Billy Graham meant when he said that his greatest fear is that God would take his hand off him.

The Holy Spirit will not produce gossip, hate, anger, revenge, envy, sensuality, lust or selfish ambition any more than a fig tree can bear an olive or a grapevine bear a fig (Js 3:12–16). It is impossible for the Holy Spirit to produce other than the fruits such as love, joy, peace and self-control.

It is scandalous – offensive to God and should be to all of us – when we worship and praise him, sit under the teaching of the word and enjoy the fellowship of believers, yet threaten the unity of the Spirit by words that reveal bitter hearts. I pray for revival. I sometimes think that revival will come when we, like those described in the early chapters of Acts, are together and have such a care for one another that we are detached from earthly and material concerns (see Acts 2:44f and Acts 4:32). This had obviously subsided by the time James wrote his epistle. I am not calling for people to sell all they own and give it away, I am only referring to the kind of care that once pervaded the earliest church.

Revival tends to change people's views about what matters. For example, just before the Cane Ridge Revival (1801) there were several denominations in Kentucky that were at each other's throats – largely over doctrine. A rival spirit prevailed with those who said 'baptism is by immersion', 'you cannot lose your salvation', 'there should be no music in the church', 'we are the true church' and things like that. Churches rejoiced when their rivals were low in attendance or when one crossed a theological line and joined them. But at the height of the Cane Ridge

Revival (I have read the original accounts) *these things just did not matter*! There was such love and mutual acceptance that rivalries and differences evaporated – that is, until the Revival subsided.

James knew what the real Holy Spirit was and what he was like. It grieved him to see a rival spirit emerge in the Jerusalem church. It should grieve all of us when we participate in scandalous worship rather than the unity of the Spirit.

# 19

# Meeting Another's
# N-E-E-D

A man finds joy in giving an apt reply – and how good is a
timely word!

*Prov. 15:23*

At Westminster Chapel I introduced a Prayer Covenant that
over three hundred members promised to pray every day,
and one of the petitions was that each of us would 'speak
only blessings into people's lives and to speak evil of no
one'. It was life-changing for all of us. Those were wonderful, wonderful days. Hardly a week went by when, in the
vestry before a service when the deacons met to pray, someone did not gently slap another's wrist with the word 'Speak
blessings!' when one expressed an annoyance over something. Often it was I who would be cautioned by one of
them! The easiest thing in the world is to be negative, to say

what you feel, to express being upset over someone's conduct or to be critical.

That Prayer Covenant was born during one of our holidays in America when I heard our friend Randy Wall give a Bible Study. He told how people can say a word in jest but which could be a little sarcastic and how it would leave a person feeling heavy for the rest of the day. I will never forget Randy's words: 'I want to speak blessings into people's lives when I speak.' He based the statement on two verses:

Let your conversation be always full of grace, seasoned with salt, so that you may know how to answer everyone.
Col. 4:6

Do not repay evil with evil or insult with insult, but *with blessing*, because to this you were called so that you may inherit a blessing.

1 Pet. 3:9

My sermon from these verses, called 'Speaking Blessings', was for a while the most ordered tape in our library.

We all need to be reminded to be positive, not to be negative, and to speak words that will make another person feel – well, just *good*. 'The tongue of the wise brings healing' (Prov. 12:18).

There are basically two kinds of people: energisers and drainers. Some people energise me! I love to be around people like that. They have a way of affirming you, dignifying you, making you feel esteemed and important and leaving you with fresh energy. There are those who – sadly, even when you see them coming – give you a heavy feeling. You know they will be critical, say something that is negative, point out what is wrong and leave you drained and in need of a rest!

What we should aim for, I believe, is to speak so as to meet another's *need*. Negative people will often say, 'If I don't say it, nobody will,' justifying their words. Of course there are times when a word needs to be said – lovingly and gently – that is negative. A lot in this book is negative, as I had to point out wrong things that certain people described in the Bible have said. Moreover, James is being negative when he calls the tongue 'a fire', or 'deadly poison'. I pray therefore that this book will be emancipating for every reader.

So when *do* you speak negatively and when do you say what is always positive? I answer: when it meets another person's true *need*. The best advice would be Jesus' words, often called the Golden Rule, 'Do to others what you would have them do to you' (Luke 6:31). Therefore *say* unto others what you would have them say to you. I have treasured words that were put to me – which could be construed as negative – as when Josif Tson said to me, 'R.T., you must totally forgive them' – a word that did not particularly bless me at the time (to put it mildly). But it set me free. That moment with Josif Tson turned out to be my finest hour. So a negative word, fitly spoken and well timed, can be a tremendous blessing. It sets one free.

But how do we know when we will have that precise effect upon another when we speak? I have come up with an acrostic, which I have applied for a number of years. It has worked many times to energise people but also to keep me from saying what I might regret. I ask myself four questions before I speak to a person, all geared to do one thing – to meet their need:

N – is it necessary?
E – does it emancipate?
E – does it energise?
D – does it dignify?

# N

The first question we need to put to ourselves is *whether it is necessary* to say something. I could have saved myself so much grief over the years had I put this question to myself before speaking: 'Do I need to say this? Is it necessary that I say this?' If I were totally honest I think that in most cases when my words backfired it was because there was no need whatever for me to say what I said.

Every minister – in public or in private – should be controlled by this question: Is it necessary to say what I am about to say? When in the pulpit one should ask – whether it be a clever word, a joke, a humorous word or even if it is theologically sound – is it really necessary to say this *now*? I know what it is to be tempted to make a statement which, if I really said it, would mean I would very possibly lose the anointing that was with me up to that moment. I will say to myself, 'But this will make them laugh,' or 'I see someone out there who needs this,' or 'Since this is good theology it can't go wrong.' I seek to justify what I am tempted to say, when I know in my heart of hearts it is not necessary to say this now. I have to do some quick thinking – in a split second. Moreover, it may seem to be a hard call to make when you are speaking on your feet before a crowd. But I have learned that if it is not *necessary* to say it, I am better off to forfeit saying it. I seldom regret what I did not say; I often regret what I did say.

I will never forget one of the worst mistakes I ever made publicly at Westminster Chapel. It came early in my ministry there, at a Communion Service on a Sunday evening. Only one week before we had launched a campaign to raise a lot of money to redecorate the Chapel and to repair the pipe organ. Being an American I wanted success overnight. I anticipated a big response at once. But the British are different! I felt that the people were not responding to the appeal as they should have and I, sadly, said so at the Communion Table. I could hear people's sighs as I spoke. I knew immediately I had made a mistake. Mercifully we all got over it, I survived and it was eventually forgotten. But my comment was *so* unnecessary. It taught me a lesson.

Most quarrels that Louise and I have had in our forty-seven years of marriage were unnecessary. They came from a little spark, such as, 'Why did you do that?', 'What did you mean by that?' or 'That comment was totally unnecessary' (which was probably an unnecessary thing to say!). Our arguments could have been largely diffused, if not avoided, had we measured our response with the question 'Is it necessary that I say this?'

When you have to say something that is dealing with a negative situation, your words still will make the difference. For example, it may be necessary to approach a person who is involved in something wrong – and you are the only person who can do something about it. If so, what you say and how you say it can determine the entire outcome. Never forget Paul's words:

Brothers, if someone is caught in a sin, you who are spiritual should restore him gently. But watch yourself, or you also may be tempted.

Gal. 6:1

The King James Version says that we should restore one 'in the spirit of meekness'. This means that you will speak in a manner that is not self-righteous. You will be saying to that person, 'I could so easily have done what you have done – I am no different from you.'

In other words, it was necessary to say something. But approaching the same person with the pointed finger in a condemning and harsh way would be totally counter-productive. If we look back on words that we regret saying it may be surprising how often you would have to admit, 'I did not need to say that at all. I wish I had not said it.'

This is what James means by being quick to listen, slow to speak, and therefore slow to become angry (Js 1:19). If we are quick to listen we will be more likely to have the presence of mind to ask ourselves, 'Is it necessary that I say this?' After all, 'a fool shows his annoyance at once' (Prov. 12:16).

This is not to imply that when one speaks when it is necessary the words will always go down well. I recall standing up in a ministers' meeting with many important churchmen present. I questioned a decision that was about to be taken. It changed my relationship with some present, but I have not regretted what I said.

Bottom line: if what you are about to say is not necessary, *don't say it*!

# E

The second question I believe we should ask is, 'Will what I say *emancipate*?' Will my word set them free? If it is necessary to say it you might suppose that it will also set them free. Possibly. But we need all four questions of this acrostic to coalesce. I would say that if what I am about to say does not set a person free it means it is not necessary to say it! I say that because, if it is not an emancipating word it is probably not a necessary word in the first place. Jesus said that it is the truth that sets one free (John 8:32). But, as we will see below, the truth must be presented in such a way as to dignify the person. It is what Paul means by 'speaking the truth in love' (Eph. 4:15).

When Paul said, 'Let your gentleness be evident to all' (Phil. 4:5), he was addressing a fairly serious church squabble in Philippi. Two strong women in the church – Euodia and Syntyche – were apparently not speaking to each other. Each of them seemed to have a personal following and a division emerged in the church. Paul pleaded with them 'to agree with each other in the Lord' (Phil. 4:2). He then appealed for all in Philippi, simply, to be gentle. The KJV uses the word 'moderation'. The Greek word *epeiekes* comes from a root word that means 'reasonable' or 'not unduly rigorous'. The idea in Hellenistic literature meant not making a rigorous stand even though you were clearly in the right. It cuts across a legalistic spirit when one feels it is right to be inflexible for truth. I would translate this word as *graciousness*.

Try 'graciousness', says Paul. It is what sets people free. It means overlooking what might vindicate you and clear your name. You put your personal vindication on hold in order to be gracious. There is nothing more emancipating for people than this.

I vividly recall when a person I knew well was very angry with me. I was certain that they were at fault. Looking back, I would still say they really were at fault. I was upset and angry with that person. My natural inclination was to register not merely disappointment but disgust with that person. I wanted them to feel guilty and ashamed. I wanted to speak in such a manner that I could say, 'Gotcha!' Mind you, it would not have emancipated them but I would have won the battle (and lost the war).

Here is what mercifully happened. I was given presence of mind. I remembered by own acrostic, N–E–E–D. I knew that the most noble thing was to emancipate this person. But I did not *want* to set them free – they didn't deserve it! But by the grace of God I did it. Here is what I said: 'I don't blame you for feeling as you do. I am not sure I would have handled things as well as you have. You certainly have a right to feel that way.' The person melted. The situation changed. Why? That person was set free from the guilt they were probably already experiencing, not to mention the guilt trip I was about to lay on them.

It is hard to set a person free when you are angry. That was my problem. I was also being very self-righteous. The dove was barely hovering over me! I was perilously close to grieving the Spirit and missing the blessing. I can only say that God was gracious to me. It was so kind of him to put my own acrostic before me in the nick of time. It also helped to encourage me to be more emancipating with my words with offended and offensive people thereafter.

I remember how someone set me free. I was angry with a particular person on the staff of a former church. I wanted to give them a piece of my mind. I also wanted other people to know what had happened. But a wise and sensible person came to me and pointed out this person's background – how deprived they were and how they were so much less fortunate than I. This friend pointed out how I would alienate this member of staff if I said what was on my mind, and how an offended brother is more unyielding than a fortified city (Prov. 18:19). I calmed down. I was set free. What this friend said to me was necessary and emancipating.

The greatest thing a preacher can do is to set people free. If one preaches under the anointing of the Spirit – and doesn't mix his words with getting at somebody, the result will be that people are set free. 'Where the Spirit of the Lord is, there is freedom' (2 Cor. 3:17). The ministry of the word is to set captives free. Some are in bondage from jealousy, some in sexual bondage, some are in legalistic bondage and some are in bondage to pleasing people. An emancipating word from God gives inner liberty, a healing inside.

*You* have the power to do this! You do not need to be a public speaker or a church leader or a Christian with a high profile to do this. You can do this with your closest friend, with those you work with, with strangers or whenever unexpectedly you have an opportunity to give a timely word.

One should seek to do this, whether speaking to hundreds, to thousands – or to one other person. Jesus did that. He set people free.

# E

The next question I would suggest we ask ourselves is, 'Will what I say *energise*?' Will my words to them provide energy, vigour and renewed ability to cope?

When I was at Westminster Chapel I always prayed for wisdom in the vestry as well as in the pulpit. It would give me enormous satisfaction when people would come in with a problem and leave feeling energised. I could not always do that, but I tried.

This may be the hardest thing of the four items to carry out. However, here is a promise: if you *try* to energise them, you will almost certainly do them no harm!

After all, part of tongue control is not to send a spark that will ignite a flame; not to utter poison that will make them sick. So when we are trying to energise, it is highly unlikely that the fire of hell will erupt.

And I can promise one more thing: if you ask yourself, 'Will what I say *energise*?', you are not likely to regret what you say to anyone – even if you don't energise them! Try to energise them, therefore, and you will not offend. Neither are you likely to make them defensive. You probably won't 'stick your foot in it' or make a comment that will upset them.

The way you energise is two-fold: (1) what you don't say, and (2) what you do say. Here is advice one can safely apply when you want to energise a person (what you don't say):

1   Make sure you say nothing that smacks of pointing the finger. Don't criticise. Somerset Maugham said that when people ask for criticism they really want praise! Most people you meet already have a fairly severe

problem with guilt. The last thing they need is to feel you are accusing them of anything. Remember, the devil is the accuser! Don't be the devil!

2   Say nothing that will make them fearful or the slightest bit intimidated. Be careful that what you say is neither threatening nor gives them a feeling of being inferior. Don't talk down to them. Most people have something of an inferiority complex, so don't add to it!

3   Do not say anything that will play on their jealousy. Do not puff yourself up. Don't name drop. Do not talk about your good news. It is easy to find someone who will weep with you; few will rejoice with you.

Here are things you can do that will help energise:

1   Let them save face. If you happen to know they have done something that is wrong, give them a way out. Dale Carnegie in *How to Make Friends and Influence People* says that if you let the other person save face you can win a friend for life! Cover for them, protect their self-esteem, don't draw attention to anything that already has them feeling guilty.

2   Think of something that will give them hope – something to look forward to. We all need something to look forward to. God made us that way; he understands that. If you can say something that is optimistic and cheerful, this is what most people want to hear.

3 Encourage them to talk about themselves. People love to talk about themselves. Let them speak freely about themselves. I learned from Alan Bell to ask people, 'Tell me your greatest pain and your greatest pleasure at the moment.' That will draw them out. When they feel you care, it gives them an energy they didn't have.

4 Ask them to let you pray with them – right there. If you sense this would make them uncomfortable, then tell them you will be praying for them. Ask them how you can pray for them – they will probably tell you. It sends a beautiful signal and gives a wonderful feeling.

Energising another person is not the easiest thing to do. But do try. And, like I said, you will spare yourself from emitting deadly poison.

# D

The fourth question you may put to yourself is, 'Will I *dignify this person* by what I am about to say?' Dale Carnegie says in his famous book, *How to Win Friends and Influence People*, that the greatest urge in the world is the desire to feel important. We all want and need significance. When we treat a person with dignity we will not start a forest fire! Forest fires caused by lack of tongue control come from demeaning a person, making them somehow feel second-class, insignificant and unimportant.

I have long been intrigued that the common people heard Jesus gladly (Mark 12:37, KJV). Why? It is because they felt affirmed and important. He spoke in a manner by which they felt he understood them. He gave them dignity, significance. Even a leper – utterly ostracised by society – knew he could get away with approaching Jesus, and was accepted and cleansed (Matt. 8:2–3).

Here are some suggestions on how you might dignify a person:

1   Give them time. We show how much we esteem a person by how much time we give them. This is not always easy to do, especially if we are busy people. But if you want to affirm a person and make them feel significant, you must take time with them.

2   Look into their eyes. Even if they do not look into your eyes, look into their eyes. A person who cannot look into someone's eyes may have a problem with guilt or confidence. Make sure you look into their eyes. They will know they have your attention.

3   Smile. At least look pleasant! When we began the Pilot Light ministry in London (witnessing in the streets to passers-by), the hardest thing in the world for me to do was to smile. But I began doing it anyway! And what do you supposed happened? More people stopped to talk and would receive my pamphlet.

4   Pay them a sincere and true compliment – if it is not contrived. Don't be phoney, they will see through that. But if you try you can find something about them that your instinct tells you they are pleased about. 'I've heard a lot about you' (if true), 'You have a wonderful smile', 'I love your accent.'

5   Ask them if they will please pray for you – perhaps not
    then, but it affirms that you believe in them. They will
    feel important in your eyes. It is possible that few people
    ask them to pray for anyone, and if you ask them, it
    gives them a higher level of significance. What is more,
    if you are like me, you need all the prayer you can get!

The bottom line is this: if you want to excel in tongue
control, speak in such a manner that meets a person's need.
You will not only be spared regrettable words; you will
actually bless people!

# 20

# The Positive Power of the Tongue

The tongue has the power of life and death, and those who love it will eat its fruit.

*Prov. 18:21*

Once at Westminster Chapel a widowed lady named Joyce came into the vestry, very distraught. Her second husband had recently died. Her first husband, whom she married when she was young, had been cruel to her and utterly rejected her. But she received love and enjoyed great companionship with her second husband. She had not been converted long and felt guilty that she, now a Christian, was going back again and again to the crematorium where she had said her final goodbye to her husband. 'I know I shouldn't do this and I feel so awful, but I have never felt so grieved.' I had not seen such distress in a long time. I felt desperate for her.

I silently cried out to the Lord on her behalf, 'Lord, please give me something for Joyce – either a word of wisdom or a word of knowledge. Give me *anything* that will encourage her. She has come to me thinking I will have a word from you.' This does not happen to me every day but a verse of Scripture suddenly came into my mind – Isaiah 54:6. I did not have the courage to ask Joyce to turn to this verse in her Bible until I had quietly read it first. As soon as I read the verse to myself I read it with her: ' "The Lord will call you back as if you were a wife deserted and distressed in spirit – a wife who married young, only to be rejected", says your God.'

'What made you read that verse to me?', she asked with amazement. (I think I was more amazed than she was.) I told her that the Holy Spirit just gave me that word seconds before and I had no idea what it said until I turned to it. A radiant smile came across her face. She was thrilled that God would do that for her. She left the vestry with great relief and joy. But I think I was as happy as she was.

'A word aptly spoken is like apples of gold in settings of silver' (Prov. 25:11), especially when such a word is perceived as directly from God to us in a time of trouble. Preaching should always do that. I am not sure mine always does that. But I want it to do that, for the truth sets people free (John 8:32) and where the Spirit of the Lord is there is liberty (2 Cor. 3:17).

I could take no credit for that word to Joyce. I had nothing whatever to do with it. But I should wish that all *my* words would do this for people – to set them free, to encourage, to affirm them and give them significance, not to mention show God's approval.

Much of this book has dealt with the negative power of the tongue. After all, most of what the Bible has to say about the tongue is negative. But I want to say as strongly as I can that it is equally true that the tongue has *positive power* – indeed, tremendous potential to bless and encourage.

It is amazing how the slightest word, whether spoken directly to us or heard second-hand, can catapult our self-image and self-esteem either towards a feeling of confidence or one of despair. In my book *Thanking God* you can read the details of how my Grandma McCurley changed a young black student's entire life by one brief sentence to him: *you have a good mind*. No one had said that to him before. She was his teacher and noted how he was so angry with the white boys who ganged up on him. He wanted vengeance upon these boys more than anything in the world. My grandmother simply told him that the best way for him to get vengeance upon those boys was for him to get a good education. He did. He later became a state senator in Illinois. At a special banquet in his honour, with my grand-mother as a special guest, he publicly affirmed those words by her to him as the turning point in his life. She vividly remembered this conversation, but had no clue that she had made such an impact on the young boy until, many years later, the senator invited her to the banquet. Our words, whether casual, intentional, serious or even in jest, can transform a person's morale.

God weighs his words with us. He often speaks to us merely to affirm us – but, sadly, we sometimes disregard it because of our low self-esteem or low estimate of our spirit-uality and walk with God. He sees in all of us a diamond in the rough. He regards us as gold that only needs to be refined. True motivation for living holy lives stems from *the way God sees us in his Son*. In fact, the biblical doctrine of justification by faith stems from the concept of 'imputed righteousness' – the way *God* sees us, not the way we see ourselves or feel about ourselves. Therefore, if God himself says something to us that affirms us, we are wise to believe him, however hard it may be at first to accept his evaluation of us.

For example, God said to Gideon, 'The Lord is with you, *mighty warrior*' (Judges 6:12). God saw Gideon as a man of valour and courage. That is not the way Gideon felt about himself. He began arguing with the Lord, but God said to him, 'Go in the strength you have and save Israel . . . Am I not sending you?' But Gideon still disagreed: 'How can I save Israel? My clan is the weakest in Manasseh, and I am the least in my family' (Judg. 6:15).

Some of us have inferiority complexes because of where we were born or brought up. Being from Kentucky might do that for a person! I grew up knowing that Kentucky was one up from Arkansas, which was once at the very bottom of the American states when it came to educational standards. In other words, Kentucky would have been at the bottom but for Arkansas. 'Thank God for Arkansas,' we used to say! But this no doubt rubbed off on me. I imagined if I said I was from Kentucky people would look down their noses at me – and some actually did.

That is the way Gideon felt. *My clan is the weakest in Manasseh, and I am the least in my family*. God saw him differently – as a mighty warrior. It was his family and background that contributed to the feeling of inferiority.

In my early years in school in Ashland, Kentucky I overheard that my teacher said about me, 'I don't think R.T.

is an A student.' I wish I hadn't heard that. I believed for years that I could never make an A. I was convinced from then on I would always be a B or C student, and I was precisely that – right through my graduation at high school and during my early years at Trevecca Nazarene College in Nashville, Tennessee. I felt 'locked' in to this fixed mentality and perception of myself for a long time.

How did I eventually get over it? Two things. First, my dad once said to me, 'You have the intelligence to become the governor of this state.' That sounded pretty good to me, even if it was Kentucky! I struggled to believe it, but I always kept it in mind. I hung on to my dad's words. Second, my professor of theology at Trevecca, Dr William Greathouse, actually treated me as if I were his peer. I don't know why, but he made me feel that I was as bright as he was. He would make it clear he valued my point of view. It gave me confidence.

The power of a positive word. 'The tongue has the power of life and death' (Prov. 18:21).

We all need encouragement. You have the power to encourage. As Dale Carnegie said, the greatest urge any of us have is the need to feel important. We should do our best to make those we meet feel important. I realise this might be a special gift, but I would challenge you to see if that gift is in you! Start making people feel important! Don't flatter them, don't be over the top. Simply look into their eyes, and treat them with respect. They will feel from you that you regard them as important.

We must do this with our children, our friends, our peers and our pastors or teachers. Can you recall a person saying a *positive* word to you that was timely and pivotal in your life at the time? I would not want you to be contrived – not for a second – but if you were to make it your goal to speak *blessings* and say encouraging things to people, you have no idea how God might use this.

I cannot urge strongly enough to parents: encourage your children, build them up, express to them that you believe they are capable, valued and can do what they set their hearts on. If I myself could turn the clock back, I would not only spend more time with each of my children but would make it my goal to instil a high level of self-confidence in them.

We must not, however, fall into the trap of flattering people or giving false encouragement. But if you can think of what is both *truthful* and encouraging to someone, say it!

This may surprise you, but I can tell you categorically that ministers, preachers, teachers, church leaders, followers, low-profile people, secretaries, dentists, doctors, lawyers, politicians, taxi drivers, computer geniuses, high-profile people and those in authority love and appreciate encouragement. This is why Paul spent most of Romans 16 mentioning people's names and often telling why they were appreciated. If you believe in the infallibility of Scripture as I do, then take seriously even Paul's non-doctrinal words. He was inspired to encourage people *by name*. Therefore read Romans 16, probably the least known chapter of that magnificent book. What a thrill it must have been to see one's name on a parchment like that or to hear that the great Apostle Paul remembered their name!

One of my predecessors at Westminster Chapel, Dr Martyn Lloyd-Jones, was possibly the greatest preacher of the twentieth century. He was not only a genius, he was a Welsh orator. Nobody could preach like him. But I happened to know for a fact that he loved an encouraging word. He used to preach for me at my little church in Lower Heyford, Oxfordshire, where I was a pastor while doing my degree at Oxford. I remember one night as we left the church and drove towards our home in Headington after he had just preached a tremendous sermon. I forgot to say anything. There was silence in the car as we drove. I somehow discerned that he was hoping for immediate feedback regarding the sermon he had just preached. I broke the silence. 'By the way, Doctor, that sermon was wonderful, you were great tonight.' The difference it made as we drove was remarkable, almost magic. He was thrilled. 'I find that very encouraging,' he replied. I knew he meant it. After I got to know him better I discovered how on target I really was that night. He loved to be told when he wrote well, preached well, looked well. Mrs Lloyd-Jones once said to me, 'Martyn loves encouragement, he thrives on it.' But most people would think he was beyond the need. Wrong. We all need encouragement.

My friend Lyndon Bowring has an interesting view about affirming a person immediately after they have spoken publicly. 'Say what is encouraging, what builds them up. Never say anything negative – save that (if there was anything to be criticised) for later,' he would always say, because 'we all need affirmation after we have preached.'

Have you encouraged your pastor lately?

One Monday morning in London I was feeling very, very low over a sermon I had preached the day before. I phoned a friend and said, 'I am not up to being the minister of Westminster Chapel, they deserve so much better.' I expected him to say something to make me feel better. His reply: 'It is a sign of God's judgement on our times that there is not better preaching these days' – virtually agreeing with me. It was *not* what I wanted! With friends like that, who needs enemies! I was devastated. Except for one thing: in the mercy of God I received a phone call the same day from someone who said that the sermon I preached on the day before was the best sermon they had ever heard and that they had never been so blessed and motivated to be a better person as a result! I can tell you, I needed that.

The quaint Nazarene preacher known as Uncle Buddy Robinson told of someone coming up to him, saying, 'Uncle Buddy, that was the greatest sermon I ever heard.' He bowed his head and prayed, 'Lord, don't let me get puffed up.' The prayer was quickly answered. Someone immediately said of the same sermon, 'That was the worst sermon I ever heard.' He prayed, 'Lord, don't let me get puffed down.'

The next and final chapter in this very book springs from a timely compliment regarding a sermon I preached on 2 Corinthians 5:13 at Westminster Chapel. There was a lady in the Chapel, well known and respected, who seldom gave out compliments. But she complimented me on that particular sermon. I was so uplifted by it that, when I looked at my notes again, I began to see more in it myself! It actually led to the chapter that follows, an encouraging teaching on when you think you've blown it.

Lack of encouragement can sometimes lead to a virtual loss of identity. In a psychiatric hospital I knew of a patient who walked up and down the aisle on his hospital floor uttering over and over again, 'Does anyone here know my name? Does anybody here know my name? Does anybody know my name?' There is often a direct correlation between mental illness and lack of self-esteem.

A person's name in Scripture was of no small importance, especially when God gave the name. For example, Abram means *exalted father*, whereas Abraham, the new name given to him by God, means *father of a great multitude*. 'No longer will you be called Abram; your name will be Abraham, for I have made you a father of many nations' (Gen. 17:5). Jacob's given name meant *supplanter* or *one who takes by the heel*. But God gave him the name Israel, *one who struggles with God*. 'Your name will no longer be Jacob, but Israel, because you have struggled with God and with men and have overcome' (Gen. 32:28).

Calling a person by name affirms them, especially if you remember their name after an initial meeting. You can sometimes win a friend for life by merely remembering their name. This is the way God speaks to us. 'Fear not, I have redeemed you; I have summoned you by name; you are mine' (Isa. 43:1).

Speaking positively, speaking blessings, speaking encouragement is often used by the Lord to get us motivated and moving. 'You can do it,' God says to us. 'Don't give up,' he raises up people to tell us. 'You have come too far to turn back now,' God says to the Hebrew Christians in so many words (Heb. 10:32–34). Indeed, 'Do not throw away your confidence; it will be richly rewarded' (Heb. 10:35).

When God called Gideon a mighty warrior there was not a shred of evidence that this was actually true about Gideon. But God saw in Gideon what he would become – and, indeed, *exactly what he became*. God named Abraham a father of many nations when he only had Isaac as the promised son. God declares what is true when we cannot possibly see it, but he also sees the end from the beginning. It is the transforming teaching of being justified by faith alone that gives us our true identity.

God told Abram to count the stars, then said to him, 'So shall your offspring be.' Abram believed it! The result: God credited Abram's faith *as righteousness* (Gen. 15:6). That became the foundation for the New Testament teaching of justification by faith. In a word, our believing the promise in the gospel counts for righteousness in the sight of God. We may not *feel* righteous. We may not *look* righteous. But God says, 'You *are* righteous' – and the way God sees us is all that matters. It is our true identity.

Therefore, having put righteousness to our credit by our trust in him, God also wants us to *accept his opinion* of us, namely, that we are righteous in his sight because the blood of Jesus Christ covers us. His opinion is the only one that is of ultimate value. It is not our reputation. It is not what parents may have said to us. It is not what peers said to us or about us years ago. It is not what a schoolteacher may have said about us. It is not what enemies say about us. It is what *God alone* says about us. He wants us not only to believe the *promise* in the gospel but believe *what he declares is true* of us once we believe that promise.

There are too many of us who believe theoretically in justification by faith, knowing we are declared right-eous by faith, but still strive to ensure our salvation by works. It pleases God when we truly believe what he says about us.

The bottom line is that God affirms us through his Son's death, and always wants to encourage us. He knows our frame and remembers that we are dust (Ps. 103:14). He therefore even sends people along to encourage us and say things that are positive so that we will have blessings, not curses, spoken to us. What is more, if you and I will speak only blessings to people from this day on, we may have a hand in transforming a life that will one day turn the world upside down.

## 21

# Laughing at Ourselves – When we Fear we've Blown it

If we are out of our mind, it is for the sake of God; if we are in our right mind, it is for you.

*2 Cor. 5:13*

I think I could write a book on this verse. I could entitle it 'Paul's Profoundest Throw-away Comment'. It was not really a throw-away comment of course. But this particular verse is stated in a manner that might give that impression! It is a verse not widely quoted, probably not even often understood. Here are six other translations:

Whether we be beside ourselves, it is to God: or whether we be sober, it is for your cause. (KJV)

Are we insane [to say such things about ourselves]? If so, it is to bring glory to God. And if we are in our right minds, it is for your benefit. (Living Bible)

If we are 'mad' it is for God's glory; if we are perfectly sane it is for your benefit. (Phillips Modern English)

If we seemed out of our senses, it was for God; but if we are being reasonable now, it is for your sake. (Jerusalem Bible)

Are we really insane? It is for God's sake. Or are we sane? It is for your sake. (Today's English Version)

If it seems that we are crazy, it is to bring glory to God. And if we are in our right minds, it is for your benefit. (New Living Translation)

I don't remember every sermon I have preached (believe it or not!). I am told that I preached approximately 3500 sermons in my twenty-five years at Westminster Chapel. But there are rare occasions (exceedingly rare) when I can remember a sermon. And my sermon on 2 Corinthians 5:13 – called 'Laughing at Ourselves' – was one of them. I was really 'chuffed' when I came down from the pulpit that day. The American equivalent I suppose would be 'tinkled pink'. Anyway, it was because I felt that I really did understand what Paul meant in these rather strange lines. What is more, seldom had I preached a word that seemed to do so much good in setting some people free! All of us have feared at one time or another that we really blew it *big time* by our foolish comments.

Why do I close my book with this verse? In a word, it is because God wants us to leave our mistakes to him – and let him sort us out. If we feel that what we said was really, really bad – don't worry! God isn't finished with us yet. And, if perchance our words were quite appropriate after all (blessed thought!), then those to whom they were spoken will have to deal with them!

This closing chapter is designed to help us not to take ourselves so seriously. We have a gracious God.

To grasp and fully appreciate this intriguing verse – 2 Corinthians 5:13 – we need to see the context of Paul's statement. Paul's relationship with the church at Corinth was very vulnerable at that time. Some evil people – usually called 'Judaizers' (Jews who professed to be Christians and who wanted to bring Gentiles under the Law) – went to Corinth to undermine Paul's ministry and influence. They largely succeeded, causing some of Paul's own converts to doubt his apostleship, authority and authenticity. He took it hard. As F. F. Bruce put it, Paul sometimes wore his feelings on his sleeves.

The reason Paul wrote what he did in 2 Corinthians 5:13 is that he had just said something that his critics might seize upon and pick to pieces. He knew he would be seen as edging close to making himself look good when he said: 'what we are is plain to God, and I hope it is also plain to your conscience' (2 Cor. 5:11). He realises this is implying that all should see that his conscience is clear before God – therefore let all take notice!

But he admittedly said this looking over his shoulder at his critics. He insists he wasn't being defensive but he was only saying what could make his supporters in Corinth justly proud of him – and give them an answer for those who had been so critical. So here is our verse in context:

> What we are is plain to God, and I hope it is also plain to your conscience. We are not trying to commend ourselves to you again, but are giving you an opportunity to take pride in us, so that you can answer those who take pride in what is seen rather than in what is in the heart. If we are out of our mind, it is for the sake of God; if we are in our right mind, it is for you.
>
> 2 Cor. 5:11–13

Whereas Paul says, 'We are not trying to commend ourselves to you again,' the critics will retort, 'You certainly *are* trying to commend yourself; you are clearly defending yourself. How stupid do you think we are? Methinks the man doth protest too much,' to alter Shakespeare's famous line.

In this book I have said that the greatest freedom is having nothing to prove. But critical people reading Paul's words will say that he obviously needs to prove himself by speaking of his conscience before God and man. He apparently thought this might make his loyal supporters feel all the better in their support of him.

But he also knows he has made himself exceedingly vulnerable. Should he have?

Paul might have taken these verses out before he let the epistle be sent. For he knew that some would say, 'There he goes again, commending himself and trying to prove that he is a genuine apostle.'

But 'No,' Paul wants to say; 'I am only doing this so that you who still believe in me can have a good reply to those who go by what is seen rather than by what is in the heart.'

Should Paul have said it?

One thing is for sure: he said it – and left it in.

But should he have taken these lines out before he sent the letter to the Corinthians?

Reader, what do *you* think? Do you believe Paul is commending himself? He says he really isn't trying to do that, that he is saying this for *them*. Do you think he is trying to win certain Corinthians back by showing how clear his conscience is before God? Is that not implicitly commending himself?

In any case, he thinks hard about it and he decides to leave this verse in – and then adds, '*If we are out of our mind* [to talk like this], *it is for the sake of God; if we are in our right mind* [if I am in fact supposed to say what I said], *it is for you.*'

He does not say whether he was right to say what he did. He just says, '*If* we are out of our mind . . . *if* we are in our right mind . . .' He leaves it open. We all can learn from this.

It is possible that the Judaizers had implied that Paul was mental. When a heated debate takes place, especially if one is losing the argument, some will accuse their opponent of being out of their mind – or mental. It's an old ploy. What we know is, Paul uses a word that can mean *insane*. The phrase 'out of our mind' comes from the Greek word *existeemi*. It was said of Jesus in Mark 3:21, that he was 'beside himself' (KJV), or 'out of his mind' (NIV).

Paul therefore says, 'If *we* are out of our mind, it is for the sake of God.' The Greek literally reads, 'If we are out of our mind, *to God.*' The translator threw in the words 'for the sake of God'. And the second part would be literally translated, 'If we are in our right mind, *for you.*'

It has to be said that what Paul declares smacks of borderline wisdom at best – and it is certainly debatable as to whether he was or was not commending himself or only helping the Corinthians. But the fact that he adds, 'If I am out of my mind to say this', shows he is open to that very possibility, that is, that what he said was perhaps not wise. I am not saying his tongue was uncontrolled, for he was obviously in control of what he was saying – and had time to delete these words had he wanted to. I am saying none the less that he *may not have been wise* to make the claim that he was not commending himself by referring to his conscience before God. Paul knows that. That is precisely why he added, 'If I am out of my mind' – that is, 'If I should not have said this . . .'

Why, at the end of the day, did Paul say these words – and why are they important to us? Paul makes himself an example of a person like you or me who has said something that is admittedly questionable – and of what we can do about it afterwards. If we are able to learn from him, it will be a wonderfully emancipating experience for all of us.

Let us suppose, for the moment, that Paul was quite wrong to say what he did about his clear conscience. We have seen that he leaves open that possibility. What does *he* do and what should *we* do when we fear we might have blown it? Paul himself simply commits it to God as if to say, 'Let God deal with me if I have blown it.' And then adds, 'If it turns out that I was right to say this – then you people will have to answer for it.'

This verse – 2 Corinthians 5:13 – has upheld me more than you could ever imagine. Would you believe that I make a point of reading it almost every day? I do! It is a most wonderful verse for those of us who realise that what we said, just maybe, was not right; that it was borderline activity, debatable conversation.

So what do I do when I wonder if what I said yesterday – or a year ago – was the right thing? I say, 'To God with it!' Or as my friend Alan Bell suggested, 'To Heaven with it!' Yes! Leave it to God! If what I said is so horrible, he will sort me out. But if it should turn out that what I said yesterday – or a year ago – was quite in order after all, the onus is on those to whom I said it to receive it.

But the fact that I might not know for sure is not all bad; it will keep me from being self-righteous if indeed I was right! I might gloat. So God sometimes lets me remain in doubt – for my own good. This simply forces me to leave the whole matter (whether I was right or wrong) to him. That will also keep me from the temptation to point the finger and say, 'So there – I *was* right, wasn't I?'

For some of us, there are some actions in the past about which we will probably never, never, never know for sure whether they were right or wrong. That is, we will never know until we get to Heaven. God also lets some things remain in suspension to keep us from taking ourselves too seriously!

And what is the best attitude to adopt from then on? We learn to laugh at ourselves. Leave it to God. Have a laugh! The truth is, God for the moment has chosen not to tell us whether what we said or did was right! We might as well laugh because crying about it won't help! If you make a choice whether to laugh or cry, why punish yourself?

Giving something over to God is a great privilege. We cast our anxiety upon him because he cares for us (1 Pet. 5:7). Once we cast our care on him – leaving our burden to the Lord – we should not look back. The highest level of proof that we really have cast our care upon the Lord is to forget the whole thing and just laugh!

People who take themselves too seriously cannot laugh at themselves. They certainly cannot bear to be laughed at. But when we don't take ourselves too seriously we will not take it so hard when we are laughed at, therefore we can enjoy laughing with them – at ourselves!

What does Paul actually have in mind when he says, 'to God'? In other words, what is Paul counting on when he says, *to God with it*?

Paul knows that God doesn't panic. He knows that God is big and powerful – not to mention magnanimous. Paul knows that God will eventually sort him out if he was wrong – and be gracious to the Corinthians as well. They too will survive. If the critics gain an upper hand for the moment, that too is OK. Perhaps Paul needs more humbling. Maybe Paul doesn't need to be seen as totally perfect in the eyes of his supporters all the time.

So why does Paul say 'to God with it'? Because he knows full well that God will have a heart-to-heart talk with him eventually. God will put his big arms around Paul and say to him, 'Paul, sorry about this my son, but you really blew it.' God is like that! By the way, God will do that with you and me too. Maybe not today or tomorrow. But God has a way of teaching us a lesson – sometimes immediately, sometimes much later, as he did with Elijah (1 Kings 19:18).

God is in no hurry to give us the slap on the wrist or the shaking of the shoulders – or whatever we may need. I just know one thing: God tends to deal with me sooner or later, and often sooner – especially if it has to do with a cross word with Louise, my children or a close friend. I am just thankful that he doesn't let me get away with things!

I have taken positions in my preaching – also stances on other matters – and I am still not completely sure what God thinks of these. I still hope he will tell me. I can think of dozens of occasions on which I said something, took a position or a stand, and received a lot of criticism – only to have God hide his face the whole time! I don't know if this means that my critics were right, if God was displeased – or not. I just know that he has hidden his face from me at times when I wanted *so much* to see his smile or feel his approval.

So what do I do when I look back on a sermon or public stance that I still am not sure about? I side with Paul: *if I was out of my mind, to God with it; if I was led by the Spirit, the people who heard it must answer for it.* In such situations I suspect I need not know for sure because, as I have said, I might take myself too seriously and gloat. So God leaves me alone, knowing I will survive.

One of the most controversial things I ever did was at a meeting of ministers several years ago when several of us watched a rather extraordinary video of Rodney Howard-Browne. Hundreds if not thousands of people in the video, listening to Rodney, were impacted by this ministry and were actually laughing their heads off! I never saw anything like it. I loved it and they all knew it. But these very 'sound', staid and sober group of preachers in the room watching the same video were frowning, groaning and, some of them, livid. While we watched this video I whispered to the very grave preacher next to me, 'You need that' – referring to the evident joy on the faces of those in the video. 'Well I do need something,' he replied. But I made no friends that night with most of those ministers, especially when I scolded them for their closed minds and obvious recalcitrance.

Was I right to rebuke them? This to me was and still is a perfect 2 Corinthians 5:13 situation. What I said to them was borderline wisdom. It is debatable whether I was prudent. But as one translation puts it: 'If we were "mad" it is for God's glory; if we are perfectly sane it is for your benefit' (Phillips Modern Translation).

I remember warning a minister who had vehemently opposed the things of the Holy Spirit. I was fairly sure it was because he did not want to risk losing his pulpit. He used to say, 'If Tom Smith [not his real name] begins to accept this stuff, then I will say it is of God.' But Tom Smith within a year of that time did accept it, but this minister was still opposed. I reminded him of the conversation. He then brought in a different person, 'If Harriet Reynolds ever accepts this, then I will say it is indeed of God.' She did within a year, but he chose to stick to his guns. I warned him very strongly. A strain has been on our relationship ever since, although we remain friends. Was I right to be so hard on him? That's another 2 Corinthians 5:13 matter. I sometimes wish I hadn't said anything at all to him; at other times I think I was right to do so.

A lady used to come into the vestry after nearly every Sunday morning service at Westminster Chapel. She came in week after week with the same old problem. I knew what the solution was the first day she came in, but, remembering that 'most people don't want their problems solved – they only want them understood' I patiently listened, nodded, prayed much the same prayer every time and sent her on her way. But after about eighteen months of this she came in after a service when (I think) I must have been in a bad mood. I can't be sure of that, but I know I decided to risk telling her what the real problem was. She never came back to the Chapel again. Was I right? I simply don't know.

Paul had a dilemma on his hands when so many people prophesied to him 'not to go to Jerusalem' (see Acts 21). He adamantly refused their prophetic words and got to Jerusalem as soon as he could. I take the view that Paul should have obeyed the prophetic words because Luke (writing under infallible inspiration) says that 'through the Spirit' (v. 4) certain disciples urged him not to go to Jerusalem. This was confirmed by Philip's daughters and Agabus. Luke himself was clearly on the side of those who prophesied to Paul. Most people think Paul couldn't make a mistake like that.

The point is, rightly or wrongly, Paul went on to Jerusalem. Little apparent good and (it seems to me) mostly trouble, followed. Fortunately the bulk of his work was accomplished by then in any case. But Paul alludes to this in his letter to the Philippians, because he knew they wanted to know how he was. His reply was, 'Now I want you to know, brothers, that what has happened to me has really served to advance the gospel' (Phil. 1:12). Fair enough. After all, all things work together for good to those who love God (Rom. 8:28).

This is the wonderful thing. *All things do work together for good to those who love God, to them who are the called according to his purpose.* The fact that something works together for good, however, is no proof that what we did at the time was right! God is gracious and makes things work together for good. He did it for Paul. He will do it for you and me. We have such a gracious God. But we must never, never, never take the fact that something eventually turns out well as a sign that we were right all along!

God does not want us to feel guilty. This is why we have Romans 8:28. As for the past, God says 'Leave it with me.'

Once we turn things over to God we can begin to smile. And laugh. And let the past be *his* problem.

So do you fear that you have blown it by your faulty words? Leave it to God. Whatever you do, don't justify yourself. If you know that you were *clearly in the wrong*, I will now address this.

What are we to do when we know for certain that we were in the wrong? Two things. First, confess it to God, and pray that God will grant genuine repentance. 'If we confess our sins, he is faithful and just and will forgive us our sins and purify us from all unrighteousness' (1 John 1:9). This is why Jesus Christ died on the cross. We must not try to atone for our sins by trying to put things right without looking to Jesus and his death. The only atonement that has value is the satisfaction Jesus' blood gave to God himself. Trust his blood – plus nothing else. But do pray for true repentance – a definite change of mind – a further confirmation that you have been forgiven and that you can hear God's voice. This means you are not stone deaf to the Holy Spirit. The confession to God is therefore not to be a perfunctory, glib acknowledgement of your failure and sin; it is with a heartfelt sorrow for your failure along with a sincere desire to please him from now on.

There is, however, a second thing to do: do your best to put it right with the person you have hurt. Tell them you are sorry. If they don't feel like forgiving you, be patient with them and let them know you can understand their feelings. It is highly unlikely you will regret it when you try to put things right with those you have hurt. Can you do this?

James 3 was not given to us merely to make us feel guilty. He wrote these soul-searching words to change lives. Therefore, when we see we have ignited the fire of hell or have spewed out poison to others, it is time to call a spade a spade – and admit your sin to them as well as to God. Tell your Heavenly Father and the one you hurt that you are very sorry indeed.

James' words are always a timely warning that we should make every effort possible to get it right when it comes to controlling the tongue. We are fools if we take his words lightly.

# Conclusion

I began this book by sharing my most 'unfavourite' verse in the Bible – Matthew 12:36, the words of Jesus: 'I tell you that men will have to give account on the day of judgment for every careless word they have spoken.'

This is a very scary word from our Lord. Does it mean that every single word we have ever uttered – pre-conversion past, post-conversion past – will be played on a video for everybody to see and hear?

Yes, if we have not repented of such words. Being forgiven means not having them brought up to us again. When I forgive people it is a commitment never to throw their wrongs up at them. It is over. It is forgotten. Not that I don't still remember them, but I make a decision never to mention it.

This is what forgiveness means – that God does not throw up what he has forgiven.

If you are saved – which means you know you will go to

Heaven when you die because your trust is in Jesus' blood not your works – it is important that you walk in the light on your way to Heaven. If a Christian falls into failing to control the tongue and does not repent, I would take the view that he or she will have to answer for that in the Final Day when they stand before God.

I close with this question: Are you saved? Do you know for sure that if you were to die today, you would go to Heaven? And if you were to stand before God (and you will) and he were to ask you (and he might), 'Why should I let you into my Heaven?', what would you say?

Suppose that you wrote on a sheet of paper what you would say to God. It would be good if you took the time right now – before finishing this brief Conclusion – to get paper and pen and write down in your own words how you would answer the question, 'Why should God let you into Heaven?'

Based upon fifty years of ministry, here are some of the most common answers I get to this question (and I have asked thousands of people):

1   I have tried to live a good life.
2   I have done my best.
3   I am a sincere person.
4   I am an honest person.
5   I believe in God.
6   I have a lot of good works to prove that I have been a good person.
7   I live by the Ten Commandments.
8   I have tried to be good to people.
9   I have been baptised.
10  I am a church member.

11 I have been confirmed.

12 I was brought up in a Christian home.

13 I give to the church and to charities.

14 I sent some missionaries some money.

15 I live by the Sermon on the Mount.

16 I believe in the teachings of Jesus.

17 I go to church.

18 I go to church at Christmas and Easter.

19 I sent money to Billy Graham.

20 I am a Baptist.

21 I am a Catholic.

22 I love God.

23 I have suffered a lot.

24 I believe in saying 'Merry Christmas' not just 'Happy holiday'.

25 I have been to the Holy Land – and had an awesome feeling.

If any or all of these possible answers coincide with what you would honestly have written down, I must say lovingly but firmly to you that you are not saved and that you are not a Christian. This is because you are trusting in good things you have done. The Bible says, 'It is by grace you have been saved, through faith – and this is not from yourselves, it is the gift of God – *not by works*, so that no one can boast' (Eph. 2:8–9).

Belief in God does not save. Even the devil believes in God – he is not an atheist! (Js 2:19). Being a church member does not save you. Good works – the best of them – will not save you. Even if you have some success in controlling your tongue, this will not save you. Good works will even hurt if you think they will help you get to Heaven.

The only way to be saved is to acknowledge that you are truly a sinner – that you have sinned before God, and you are sorry for your sins. You must acknowledge that God sent his Son – Jesus Christ, the God-man – to live a perfect life for you and die for you. You must recognise that Heaven is a gift of God – a gift that must be received before it is yours. You receive this gift by transferring your trust in your good works to what Jesus Christ did for you on the cross. You receive this gift by faith. Saving faith is more than calling on God when you are in need or in trouble. The faith that saves is when you put 'all your eggs into one basket' – namely, the blood of Jesus. To help you I would ask you to pray this prayer:

> Lord Jesus Christ, I need you. I want you. I am sorry for my sins. I believe that you are the Son of God, that you died on the cross for my sins. I believe that you rose from the dead. I renounce hope in my good works. Wash my sins away by your blood. I welcome your Holy Spirit into my heart. As best as I know how, I give you my life. Amen.

If you prayed that prayer, share it with one other person. For here is the greatest thing you can ever do with your tongue. 'If you *confess with your mouth*, "Jesus is Lord," and believe in your heart that God raised him from the dead, you will be saved' (Rom. 10:9). Begin to pray every day. Read the Bible every day. Find a church where the Bible is preached and Christ is honoured and get involved in that church. Grow in grace by walking in all the light God gives you (1 John 1:7). And remember that Jesus said, 'I am with you always, to the very end of the age' (Matt. 28:20).

May the blessing of God Almighty – Father, Son and Holy Spirit – be with you and abide with you now and forever more. Amen.